VIRAL LEADERSHIP

VIRAL
LEADERSHIP

The Secret to Exponential Performance Improvement

Jorge A Acuña

ISBN: 0692501770
ISBN 13: 9780692501771

INTRODUCTION

Optimism is infectious, and opportunity irresistible. Progress follows progress. Someone, even government, just has to get it started.
—GLORIA MACAPAGAL-ARROYO

Have you met a supervisor, a manager, or a leader in your organization who left a great impression on you? Did his or her example lead you to improve in some way? Were the qualities of this person so infectious that they have passed through you and on to those around you? In other words, has this person's greatness gone viral?

Scientists today are creating viruses that can cure malaria, cancer, and many other illnesses. Imagine what would happen if we could create a virus that could help people feel stronger, happier, and smarter. In a way, we can. The concept of viral leadership is simple. Great leaders live the principles of excellence, and those around them can't help but learn from them and mimic their examples.

It is like a viral infection passed from patient zero—or, in this case, leader zero—to the rest of the team. "Patient zero" is the individual who begins an epidemic—from whom it spreads. "Leader zero" is at the source of a viral vaccination that brings a team from poor performance into amazing performance.

Those team members infected by leader zero continue to communicate this positive infection down the line to their peers, frontline employees, contractors, and, ultimately, to customers. Look at some of the symptoms caused by working with a great leader: open communication, mutual respect, and mutual admiration on the job.

Now imagine yourself as leader zero and passing on these traits to the rest of your team and even to your customers. Do you remember a time when you were a completely happy customer thanks to the great service you received from a firm's employees? Could you tell that those employees worked in a caring workplace and within a nurturing culture? Could you lead a team to provide its customers the same experience?

Such an impact is extremely important to understand, because viral leaders are not always great leaders. Some leaders are, in fact, terrible and treat everyone poorly. Their type of infection causes team members to act terribly toward peers and eventually toward customers too. The only viable vaccine for poor leadership is not just a great leader, but a great viral leader.

With a negative infection in the workplace, people leave in search of something better. Can you remember the last time you left a store or an office completely upset because its employees and managers were simply terrible toward you or toward one another? Can you recall a job that you left because of bad leadership? Are you in one now?

There are also very ineffective leaders, the ones who can't infect anyone with anything. They are passive and often blame others for not being able to accomplish anything. These people are not viral; they're terminal. They have nothing to offer.

When you look at happy customers and engaged employees, you can usually trace that kind of success back to a source: leader zero, the one person or team of leaders who spreads the infection of positive attitudes and practices across the entire organization. The questions we want to ask ourselves are these: How contagious are we? What kind of effect do we have on those around us— positive or negative? What kind of outbreak do we want to start today?

OUR INTENT

The intent of this work is to help new and experienced managers become leader zeros and to go viral with excellence. It aims to help:

- emerging leaders as they move into their first management roles, so they are prepared to become great leaders on the path of excellence;

- experienced leaders who feel validated in what they do well but are unsure about the principles of excellence or want refresher training on them; and
- entrepreneurs in search of new and creative ways to inspire teams.

In short, we want to help both emerging and experienced leaders gain new, creative, and critical skills to manage and lead successfully.

While this work does not cover every single scenario or industry, it is meant to give new managers in any company across the globe a solid starting point from which to prepare for their roles. It can also help seasoned managers who have taught themselves leadership and management skills and wonder whether or not they are on the right path. Here, they can find validation for what they already do well. This work can also help experienced managers explore new and creative concepts that can help them improve the performance of their younger and less experienced team members.

The skills, traits, and resources discussed here are also important for entrepreneurs who manage teams and can help these entrepreneurs become viral leaders who multiply the impact of their leadership skills exponentially.

This book is divided into two major parts. The first is about how to achieve the next level of leadership performance from emerging leaders. The second part is a field guide with tools and resources to improve personal and team effectiveness at work.

PART I

CHAPTER 1

WHY THIS, AND WHY NOW?

Be the change you want to see in the world.
—MAHATMA GANDHI

DANGEROUS PROMOTIONS

Imagine a scenario where two individuals, Eric and Laura, venture into their first work experiences. Both of them are excited to start their first jobs. Eric is a computer-network systems installer, while Laura takes on an entry-level chemical-engineering position with the same company. Like most people, they like to dream big and hope to eventually be promoted into management roles.

What happens next can happen to anyone in any role. Keep in mind that Eric and Laura represent any two people in the world in any career. They could be a teacher and a sales representative or a mechanic and a nurse.

Both Eric and Laura want better lives and have big dreams. They work hard, make sacrifices, and, most importantly, manage to build great relationships with their customers, peers, and supervisors. In time, both prove to be very motivated and ready to take on additional responsibilities.

Thanks to their efforts, Laura and Eric get their first promotions. Eric is assigned to manage the security of the division's top website. This is a high-profile role that protects customers' data and the company's reputation. Laura is transferred to new-product development. She now has an important job where she is involved in testing and designing new products.

While both are very happy with their first promotions, their new jobs ask them to specialize in the skills they already have or have learned on the job. At the core of their new positions, they are still practicing similar competencies as before, just at a higher degree of mastery. While it takes a little time for them to feel fully comfortable after their transitions, they adjust to their new roles with relative ease.

Let's take a look at them a year or two later. Laura and Eric are now at the top of their games. Laura's engineering skills are noticed by upper management. They decide to make her the department manager in the new-products division. Eric is also promoted to a management position in the computer-services department, overseeing network security.

Laura and Eric are excited about their promotions and share the news within their social networks. But suddenly, they realize something. Prior to their promotions, they were stars. Highly motivated and skilled at their past jobs, they managed to stand out. But now, in their new jobs, they don't have the opportunity to do all the hands-on things they used to excel at. This is when they begin to feel a little uncomfortable.

It becomes clear to them that they are now venturing into areas requiring expertise in competencies they have never explored before. They will be responsible for managing people and teams, not just timelines and projects.

They also realize that while they are responsible for the overall results in their respective areas, they now have to rely on the quality of work of others, not just their own. The situation makes them realize they have to develop leadership skills that are much different than those they have learned before. In the past, they needed to demonstrate that they had initiative. Now they need to motivate others to show initiative.

To complicate matters further, they begin to wonder if their relationships with their peers will change and, if so, how. It is at that moment that Eric and Laura realize that they are no longer stars and that there is much to learn and prepare for.

Let's step back to appreciate the magnitude of their dilemmas. They both spent countless hours learning the academic and technical skills they needed to get the jobs they wanted. Once they got the jobs, they specialized and refined their knowledge and skills to the point where they stood out above the rest. Laura became a better chemist, while Eric became a better IT-security professional.

Now, as a reward, they are put in positions where there are high performance expectations placed on them. However, their new roles require skills and experiences they have not yet acquired or prepared for. To meet minimum expectations, they need to learn and implement a lot of new skills in a relatively short time. From conducting interviews to motivating others, they have an entire world of knowledge to master.

But how do they learn how to best manage a team? And how do they learn what makes a team perform at top level? "You're a great team member and a smart person. You'll figure it out soon enough" is all they hear from their own managers.

When they solicit ideas from experienced managers, they hear a list of experiences and approaches that often seem to contradict each other. Some managers rule with an iron fist, enforcing every rule in the book, while others prefer a far more casual approach. Which approach is right? To make things worse, some approaches sound clearly outdated.

This situation is frightening to both Eric and Laura. In their minds, they are uncertain and have many questions and concerns. "I have never had to hire anyone before. What if I make the wrong choice? Am I still allowed to be friends with my former teammates even though I am their supervisor now? How does that work? And what do I do with those who I know don't perform like they should? I have never fired anyone. What will I do if it comes to that?"

While some organizations provide management and leadership training, most don't. Many companies assume you'll learn what you need on the job. In a 2013 Learning4Managers.com survey, 42 percent of participants stated that they taught themselves how to conduct interviews, 37 percent taught themselves how to manage conflict, and 31 percent taught themselves how to manage low-performing staff.

Without formal training, there is no guarantee that these managers are using a structured approach to management. Many of them learn by using trial and error, which represents a serious legal exposure problem for the company. Imagine the impact on the organization if one of these self-taught managers decides to ask questions during interviews that clearly discriminate against a racial or ethnic group, for example, simply because that is how they used to do it at his or her former organization. Furthermore, it is likely these people lack knowledge of industry standards and best practices, leading to wasted resources and inefficiency.

Now imagine the impact this situation has on the teams these self-trained managers oversee. If the managers are not well prepared to handle such basic functions as hiring and managing conflict, what results should we expect? When we look at this state of affairs closely, we are not surprised to hear people say that employees don't leave their jobs, but rather their managers.

Let's get back to our friends Laura and Eric. In time, and after a lot of struggles, they learn how to become good managers and leaders. One day at lunch, Eric and Laura meet and talk about their experiences as relatively new managers. They both recognize that they still have a lot to learn and that it would have been easier if they'd had some kind of resource or training for new managers during their transitions.

They also realize that many of their more seasoned peers struggle with using old-fashioned and untested methods of leadership and management with new teams. Many of the old techniques and strategies simply don't work with today's workforce. Eric and Laura wish there were training programs available to their more experienced peers so they could tune up and update their leadership and managerial skills.

Every year, new managers are promoted into their roles because they were highly skilled at their jobs as paralegals, customer-service representatives, heavy-equipment operators, and so forth. The promotion into management is almost an expectation for many. We are taught that if we work hard and are the best at what we do in our departments, our reward is to "move up the ladder" into management and leadership positions.

The problem is that being a star at your job now does not mean that you have developed the right competencies to be a star as a manager and a leader. Furthermore, just because you have been a manager for many years does not mean that the set of skills and competencies that you have taught yourself over the years are the best ones or even the right ones.

A similar scenario prevalent in many companies is the hiring of people with leadership or management experience under the assumption that they have learned the necessary skills elsewhere. But how do you know what exactly they learned and how transferable those skills are to your own team context?

A COMMON FAILURE TO LEAD AND MANAGE

> *Two crabs came out from their home to take a stroll on the sand.*
> *"Son," said the mother, "you are walking very ungracefully. You should*
> *try to walk straight forward without twisting from side to side."*
> *"Yes, Mother," said the young crab. "If you start walking*
> *straight and show me, I will follow your example."*
> —ADAPTED FROM "THE TWO CRABS," BY AESOP

Having identified that you desire knowledge on leadership, you begin to search for it. One of the most logical places to look is up the ladder of leadership so you can learn from the examples you see there. The problem is that not everyone has an ideal example to follow on their own leadership team. To illustrate this fact, let's explore a situation that has been all too familiar for many of you at some point in your careers.

A top leader and the senior board call a meeting to do what they believe they should: provide their work teams with the leadership's vision for the company. At the meeting, the top leaders use lots of metaphors and images of a positive, bright, and prosperous company future. They close by saying something like this: "We have shared with you the vision we have. We hope all of you are inspired, because without you, none of this is possible."

All is well until it's time to explain how the company will reach this level of prosperity. In some cases, that task is left to the managers (including you) and the team leaders. If you get a more precise answer, you usually hear some sort of equation that contains goals based on a target that needs to be met by a multiplier within some time frame. For example, the leaders say, "To make this vision come true, we will need to double [multiplier] the number of customers [target] over the next year [time frame]." Note that by "we," they often mean *you*.

At first, it sounds like they have just provided you a SMART goal: it is specific, measurable, apparently achievable, and realistic (at least in the minds of the leaders), and it has a defined timeline that determines by when it needs to be accomplished. But there is a problem. You still don't know *how* the goal should be accomplished.

The lower-ranking managers and leaders are now left with a lofty goal. But they have no direction for achieving it. Should they ask? What if asking questions makes them look like they are being difficult and are not team players? What if seeking clarification makes them look and feel incompetent? But without clear direction, what will they do?

Remember Eric and Laura? Imagine them now in this situation. Their performances will now be evaluated based on results they may or may not feel they have control over. And with these insecurities in their minds, they now have to lead teams without the expertise to do so. Do you think they are under enough pressure yet?

In the midst of this dilemma, they are now primed to fall victim to the most common pitfalls for managers. These are some of the tell-tale signs of a negative viral leader:

- They try to force people to do more with less.
- They revert back to production mode instead of leadership mode.
- They give up hope and decide to do nothing.

None of these responses help people like Eric and Laura feel like they are accomplished professionals on their way to stardom in their current roles. How will they become the kind of positive viral leaders their teams will admire and support?

Sending people into management or leadership roles without providing them with a real picture of what to expect and sending them to work without the right tools is simply negligent. This is a harmful business practice, and it is unfair to both the person being promoted as well as to the teams and individuals he or she will work with.

CHAPTER 2

HOW PREPARED ARE YOU TO BECOME A VIRAL LEADER?

What you are speaks so loudly I can't hear what you are saying.
—RALPH WALDO EMERSON

As a leader and manager, there are three critical conversations you'll have with the team members you work with:

1. The initial interview that takes place when you both decide to work together
2. Performance conversations that take place when you motivate, redirect, and correct
3. The conversations you have in the midst of conflict

One of the key tasks of this book is to prepare you for these conversations and equip you with the skills viral leaders use to maximize effectiveness. Before embarking on this journey, we should explore what managers and leaders know and how they gained this knowledge.

In 2013, Learning4Managers.com issued a survey on learning competencies for supervisors and managers. In the survey, managers were asked how they learned critical management skills, certain of which we believe a viral leader should master to create and nurture high-performing teams. Respondents to the survey were presented with a list of key skills and shared with us how they learned them. The skills could be:

- Self-taught
- Learned in school
- Learned on a previous job
- Learned in their current workplace
- Not applicable

Let's review the latest analysis of the findings.

1. LEARNING INTERVIEW SKILLS

One of the competencies we asked about was conducting interviews. Attracting and hiring the right staff is the first key step toward building strong and successful teams. Making a bad hire can also mean many hours of conflict, stress, and difficulties for the team.

Identifying who the star performers are among the many candidates who are interviewed and getting the right people on board is no easy task. You would expect organizations to make it a priority for managers and supervisors to be well prepared in this area. However, we found that organizations might not be doing a great job at preparing hiring managers for the task.

CONDUCTING INTERVIEWS

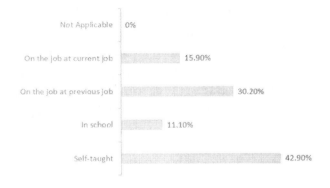

Our survey reveals that nearly one in ten managers learned this skill in school. The rest are almost equally divided between those who claim to have learned the skill on the job or at a previous job and those who have been self-taught. These numbers are in line with anecdotal reports from the many managers and supervisors we have worked with over the years.

Professor Lauren Rivera at Northwestern University Kellogg School of Management identified that interviewers tend to rely on their own images of cultural fit to determine if a candidate should be hired or not. The Price Group in Texas found that 90 percent of the owners of five hundred small businesses nationwide decide on a job applicant based on a gut feeling and have no formal hiring-assessment process.

In many countries around the world, this is of particular concern because there are many laws and regulations that directly affect the hiring process. Courses on topics like discrimination should be mandatory training for managers and supervisors before they begin conducting interviews. Refresher courses should be offered on a regular basis to ensure adherence to best practices.

In countries where regulations about interviewing and hiring are mission critical to corporations, without a clear understanding and training on how to implement these regulations, companies may be at risk of missing out on the most talented staff or even be at risk of being in noncompliance with the law. Such is the case in the Middle East, for example, where nationality and gender considerations are critical. In some Middle East countries, men are not allowed in some women's clothing stores—as employees or customers. Some companies in the region are only allowed to hire a certain number of people from other countries. These regulations may seem foreign and even unfair to people from other regions, but they must be followed to maintain compliance with local governance.

2. LEARNING TO CONDUCT PERFORMANCE REVIEWS

Not every organization performs annual or periodic reviews, but in those that do, employees often feel that they are put into situations where they are judged unjustly. Many leaders feel that reviews are a waste of time or an exercise in futility—hardly what a viral leader wants to spread.

The initial survey results indicate that about 40 percent of the surveyed managers learned to conduct performance reviews at their previous jobs. About a quarter of the remaining surveyed report having been self-taught, and another quarter learned how to conduct performance reviews at their current jobs.

CONDUCTING PERFORMANCE REVIEWS

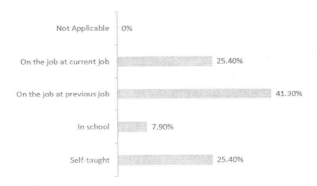

Not Applicable	0%
On the job at current job	25.40%
On the job at previous job	41.30%
In school	7.90%
Self-taught	25.40%

With 41.3 percent of their managers learning to conduct performance reviews elsewhere, organizations don't always think it necessary to evaluate and assess how they do it. In fact, leaders often make the mistake of *assuming* that experienced managers have learned skills elsewhere. This is one of the reasons that these managers are felt to be so valuable to the company. The company believes that it is saving itself the cost and time to train the managers and relies on their prior work experience.

While experience is important, different organizations may have different cultures and ideas of how to conduct reviews. This can lead to confusion and tension during the review process. Imagine a company with two managers. One is taught at a previous job that performance reviews are an opportunity to reward good work. The other learned at a previous job that reviews are an opportunity to point out flaws. This lack of consistency can lead to frustration among the employees.

To maintain employee engagement, the organization must invest in standardizing and retraining managers to ensure that they use an approach that supports motivation, engagement, and better performance. The approach used must match the corporate culture as well as the needs of the employees.

3. LEARNING CONFLICT-MANAGEMENT SKILLS

A report published by the Bureau of Justice Statistics, a section of the US Department of Justice, indicates that a high number of employees in the private sector report being victimized by people they work with.

Over 28 percent of men and nearly 40 percent of women report being victims of violence in a relationship at work, such as with a customer, a patient, a supervisor, an employee, or a peer. Out of all of these, the coworker-violence frequency appears to rate the highest.

Surveys by many different groups across the years indicate that managers spend 10 to 26 percent of their time managing conflict in the workplace. As an average, this accounts for a full day each week. As disturbing as these numbers may appear, there is an underlying concern they do not clearly reveal.

Nearly 6 percent of managers who successfully brought conflict to a resolution report that it took over ten days to resolve the issue in their recent situations. Add this to the fact that nearly half of the managers dealing with conflict report that it has a negative impact on productivity within their organizations.

These alarming numbers make us quickly realize that conflict is costly and has long-lasting effects. Since ignoring workplace conflict only allows it to prolong lost productivity, our only viable option is to manage the conflict quickly and effectively. Better yet, we can learn how to identify its early signs and prevent it altogether.

Clearly, preparing managers and leaders to manage and prevent conflict must be a priority. However, we found that companies are not exactly giving this topic the attention it deserves when it comes to training.

We asked managers how they learned to manage conflict. The majority of them—to the tune of 36.5 percent—indicated having learned this skill in a previous job. This answer was followed by 38.1 percent who claimed to have been self-taught. At a current job and at school were the next highest-ranking choices at 12.7 percent each.

It is worth noting that no manager considered this skill not applicable in the survey, which underlines the importance of knowing how to deal with conflict in today's workplace.

What raises concern is that almost four of every ten managers claim to be self-taught on this subject. This implies that they do not count on the support of formal training in conflict management and may be exposing themselves and their organizations to serious consequences.

CONFLICT MANAGEMENT SKILLS

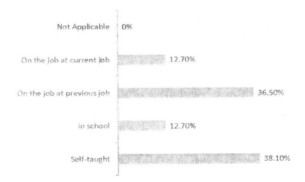

The results also indicate that managers today are approaching the matter in the same way managers have done for years: doing the best they can without formal support, training, or standard methods. This approach can lead to serious problems at work. With nothing but anecdotal information to go by, managers may be unknowingly fostering or ignoring ongoing conflict, which could escalate into bullying or violence.

Leaders and managers come into conflict situations almost daily. The conflict can be with superiors, peers, with those they supervise, or with vendors and clients. If these conflict situations are not well managed, they can easily escalate into more serious matters. An argument between a manager and a vice president can lead to ongoing resentments and loss of productivity. A feud between departments can lead to lost productivity. Workplace bullying can lead to low motivation and frustration. A disgruntled employee or customer might escalate the issue into a full-blown fight and put the entire organization in the midst of a legal battle. In the worst cases, we have seen in the news acts of unbelievable violence sometimes caused by poor conflict-management skills.

If managers are not sufficiently prepared to manage these situations or are left to their own resources (and again, nearly four out of ten indicate that they are), we are putting our organizations and the people in them at risk.

Participate in the survey! Follow this link: **http://viralleaders.com/?p=41**

PREPARED FOR VIRAL LEADERSHIP?

The items covered in the survey are only a few aspects of management and leadership, and yet we can see already how ill prepared many individuals are to handle relatively common expectations. How prepared do you feel to take charge?

Perhaps you are ready, but you haven't been able to find validation yet. Perhaps you suffer from impostor syndrome and feel like you are not deserving of your accomplishments because you simply don't know if what you are doing is the right thing.

One of our goals is to help you identify how you can develop into a viral leader and to strengthen the areas in which you already perform as one. The secret to successfully becoming a viral leader is in you. Be honest with your self-assessment of your skills and attitudes, and you'll get a true and clear picture of where you are and what it will take for you to transform into the kind of viral leader you want to become.

CHAPTER 3

BECOMING A VIRAL LEADER— THE JOURNEY AHEAD

The Wind and the Sun were arguing over which one of them was stronger. When they saw a traveler coming down the road, they agreed on a way to decide their dispute. Whichever of them could make that traveler take off his coat would be regarded as the stronger of the two. The Sun hid behind a cloud and the Wind began to blow as hard as it could. The harder it blew, the more tightly did the traveler wrap his coat round him. Finally, the Wind had to give up in despair. Then, the Sun came out and kissed the cheek of the traveler with the heat of summer. The traveler quickly found it too hot to walk with his coat on.
—ADAPTED FROM "THE WIND AND THE SUN," BY AESOP

The story of the Wind and the Sun reminds us that trying to force people into action is often a lose-lose proposition. At best, you'll spend a significant amount of effort and resources to get minimal results and make everyone unhappy. On the other hand, if we learn how to motivate others in ways where they can see a benefit to them, we will get results that maximize our strengths and resources.

To help emerging and experienced leaders become viral leaders and gain critical skills to manage and lead successfully, we must first explore, and perhaps challenge, our own views regarding these two central concepts: leadership and management.

To Lead or to Manage? That Is the Question

Many professionals like to start academic arguments trying to distinguish the fundamental differences between a leader and a manager. In some cases, the true reason for the argument is simply a matter of ego. Some people want to give one role greater importance than the other as a means to make themselves seem more appealing or needed. This sort of argument creates a rift between the two roles and their functions and misleads people into thinking that they can exist in complete isolation from each other. This approach can be deceiving and harmful to individual and team performance.

A quick search through social-media sites easily reveals graphics and posters portraying a stark contrast between leaders and managers. However, if you pay close attention, you may realize that what they often actually compare is the difference between a *good* leader and a *bad* manager, or vice versa. These are not fair comparisons and serve only to undermine the fact that leadership and management indeed go hand in hand.

If we carefully observe the work and lives of the best managers and leaders, we soon learn that few successful leaders can achieve greatness without sound managerial skills, and few managers can be truly effective without a wide range of leadership skills. More importantly, if you want to establish a competitive advantage as either a leader or a manager, you'll need to excel at being both—to become a great viral leader.

If we are willing to admit that leadership and management are not like oil and water but that they work together and enhance each other, then we can benefit from the greatest advantages of each. The relationship between leadership and management is symbiotic; they benefit and support each other. Once we come to that realization, we can begin to leverage our strengths more effectively.

To start, let's define what a leader and a manager are within the context of our discussion.

The Ideal Viral Leader

To define the roles of leaders and of managers, we'll borrow a page from the ancient Greek philosophers. They defined virtues by the qualities they would have in an ideal world. So, to define management and leadership, we'll start by imagining the highest standard or ideal that each of the two words represent.

This approach is not unlike setting a vision for a company. We do not settle for a vision based on what has been achieved. Instead, we create a vision based on the ideal of what the company could become. Today, a similar approach is used in leadership-coaching systems.

Through coaching, individuals identify who they are in relationship to their careers and their positions by exploring the ideal first. Only then do we set goals and objectives. As a result, we ensure that we are not settling for anything else but the very best.

With this idealistic mentality, let's consider what some of the traits of ideal leaders and managers would be. How would you define an ideal manager and an ideal leader? Start by thinking of those people who you know and admire who display ideal traits. What were their best traits as managers and as leaders? Were there traits that are applicable only to managers? Were there some only for leaders? What kind of manager and leader would you like to be?

In your opinion, what are the qualities of the Ideal Leader and the Ideal Manager? Share your thoughts online:

http://viralleaders.com/book-companion-toolkit/ideal-leader/
http://viralleaders.com/book-companion-toolkit/ideal-manager/

Here are some of the questions you may want to consider when identifying ideal leaders and managers.

- Recall the best leader or manager you ever encountered. What was that person like?
- What were the top three qualities that made this person the best in your eyes?
- How did this person communicate goals to the team and to individuals?
- How did this person lead successful team meetings?
- What did this person do to motivate teams to perform better?

WORKING DEFINITIONS

The older I get, the less I listen to what people say
and the more I look at what they do.
—ANDREW CARNEGIE

A key concept for us to consider at this juncture is that we can measure ideal leadership and management by their results. They are like the wind: we can't see it, but we can see its effects on the world around us. And, if we learn to harness and master the energy behind ideal leadership and management like the wind, we can maximize our results.

After discussing this topic with hundreds of individuals, we attempt here to summarize their observations on the key characteristics behind ideal leadership and management. We'll use these observations as the basis for our working definitions throughout the book.

THE IDEAL LEADER

We'll start with a comprehensive definition of the ideal leader and then explain each component in detail. When we try to define what an ideal leader is, we are really trying to define the leader's mission. A mission is what makes unequivocally clear what this person is all about.

For example, when you look at an ambulance or a police car, you know exactly what that vehicle is for and what the crew within it does. When you look at pilots in uniform, you have a very clear idea of what their missions are. The definition of an ideal leader will help us create that level of clarity about what we want to become.

Definition: Leaders are stewards of trust. They endeavor to inspire individuals to set their unrealized potential free. Leaders help individuals pursue excellence through action. Leaders bring people together to form teams and instigate members of those teams to manifest their maximum performance through uninhibited synergy and teamwork. Leaders empower teams to act in relentless pursuit of a cause with purpose.

Let's take a detailed look at the key aspects of the definition.

STEWARD OF TRUST

Trust is the beginning of any kind of relationship. Without trust in each other, leaders and teams cannot move forward effectively. When you think about it, we only buy from people and brands we trust. We also choose to ask for advice from people we trust.

The ideal leader is a person who earns and maintains trust. Trust is what makes it possible for followers to want to be led by the viral leader. An ideal leader also helps people feel trusted and dependable.

INSPIRATION

In ancient mythology, a muse was a being that inspired artists to create music and poetry. In business, leaders are like muses in that they bring inspiration to their teams. Leaders don't always do the work, but they inspire people to do their best work and to be creative.

Inspiration is about leaders painting a true and attractive picture of the future. When they do this, people don't fear exploring the unexplored, innovating, or trying what has not been tried before. People feel free to become better versions of themselves, thanks to the inspiration of a leader.

EXCELLENCE THROUGH ACTION

Leaders help people to expect the best from themselves. The ideal leader understands that while perfection isn't realistic, excellence is. They do not expect perfection but rather that each person seek to give the best of themselves to the task at hand.

This expression of excellence happens through actions. Leaders motivate people to want to showcase their best work and feel proud of it. Those following the ideal leader feel compelled to act and do their absolute best to accomplish what is needed.

INSTIGATOR OF MAXIMUM PERFORMANCE

While leaders use inspiration as a passive call to action, viral leaders are also proactive in motivating action. People who follow viral leaders don't have time to waste. They give not only their best; they give it their all. Productivity under viral leaders is always higher than under others.

UNINHIBITED SYNERGY AND TEAMWORK

Teams working for great leaders have the ability to leverage their diversity into cohesiveness, resulting in synergy and a great teamwork experience. This synergy is unbound or unrestrained. When everyone works together toward the same goal and leverages each other's strengths, the impact of their effort multiplies exponentially. Competition is encouraged as long as it is constructive and not disruptive. Ideal leaders also help remove all external obstacles to this synergy.

RELENTLESS PURSUIT OF A CAUSE WITH PURPOSE

Under the guidance of an ideal leader, the team sees only one option: success. This does not mean it will not encounter adversity or will not experience failure. The team simply won't settle for failure, and it will continue to push forward until it gets the result it seeks. Failures are nothing but learning steps. To the determined leader, failure is how we refine our approach to success.

Individuals on the team want to know that what they do has value. They want to feel that they are becoming a better people by what they do and pursue. An ideal leader helps them see the true value of their work and how important each member is to the overall results.

What other characteristics would you add to the definition of the ideal leader? Share your thoughts online at: http://viralleaders.com/book-companion-toolkit/ideal-leader/

THE IDEAL MANAGER

Once again, we will work on trying to identify the mission of an ideal manager. We will try to ascertain what characteristics define the ideal manager and set the role apart from others.

Definition: Managers are stewards of assets who find the right mix of tools, assets, time, people, resources, and materials to turn seemingly impossible challenges into successes. Managers are the champions that teams count on to get the job done.

Let's take a closer look:

STEWARD OF ASSETS

The principal idea of management is the ability to organize and utilize wisely what one has been given in order to achieve an outcome. Managers are entrusted to oversee the best use of all the resources at their disposal.

The ideal manager looks at all assets and resources (people, time, etc.) as if they were pieces of a puzzle and arranges them to create a coherent picture. Managers ensure that the pieces stay in place and rearrange them as needed to create an evolving picture that keeps up with the demands of the job. Managers also ensure that the right mix of resources is being used for maximum efficiency, preventing resource waste and shortages.

In a way, managers are like alchemists from ancient times. Alchemists had the goal of mixing different elements in order to create gold. At the time, the task was impossible. But alchemy gave birth to modern chemistry, and today we can synthesize almost anything.

A manager, like an alchemist, tries to find the right mix of assets to achieve what may at first appear as an unattainable goal.

CHANGE AGENT

Great managers are not expected to simply follow directions and keep the corporate engine running. They are change agents who continuously look for ways to improve current processes.

Change happens, and ideal managers are ready for it. In fact, ideal managers are ready to make changes as needed in order to achieve objectives. They are flexible and adaptable and help their teams maneuver through transitions.

CHAMPION

The manager is there to support both the cause and the team. Managers stay engaged and help others stay engaged and on task.

Teams working under great managers will tell you how they see their managers as champions of their causes. Leaders who appoint great managers to projects will tell you how those managers are also champions to *their* causes. A great manager is seen by everyone as the person who finds the best balance to achieve goals.

What other characteristics would you add to the definition of the ideal manager? Share your thoughts online at http://viralleaders.com/ book-companion-toolkit/ideal-manager/

TODAY'S EXPECTATIONS OF IDEAL LEADERS AND MANAGERS

Clearly, managers are expected to be much more than drones supervising the comings and goings of workers and keeping track of inventory. Leaders are expected to do much more than simply sit back and watch commands being obeyed. Today's business environment demands much more from both the leadership and the management functions. Furthermore, viral leadership requires us to step up and elevate our expectations.

The characteristics we listed for leaders and managers are the foundations required to make a leader and a manager effective and successful at their jobs. However, to excel, managers and leaders need to adopt characteristics from each other's descriptions.

As we noted earlier, for managers to excel, they need to be good leaders. This means they need to evolve into manager-leaders. In a similar way, leaders need to be good managers, and therefore, they need to evolve into leader-managers. To simplify these terms, we'll simply call the leader-manager and the manager-leader roles the viral-leader role. We call this quality "virality," a term coined by Learning4Managers to describe the qualities of a positive and effective viral leader.

CHAPTER 4

VIRAL LEADERSHIP: A TARGET IN MOTION

Trust men and they will be true to you: treat them
greatly and they will show themselves great.
—RALPH WALDO EMERSON

PURSUING THE IDEAL

Now that we have these working definitions, how do people become ideal, viral leaders? To explore this question, let's take a look at what exemplary leaders and managers do to achieve their goals. Once you learn to do what they do, you'll be equipped to share with your teams how they can do the same.

SETTING EXPECTATIONS

Before anyone can become truly effective at leading a team to success, he or she must set a very clear picture of what is expected of the team and each individual within it. As a starting point, let's take a look at what is expected of you, not as a leader or a manager, but simply as an individual first.

You've probably heard people say "I didn't think I had it in me" after they accomplish a difficult task. Perhaps someone completed a project much earlier than expected, or perhaps the task tested his or her strength beyond perceived limits. It is as if people are surprised by their own results—and more so when the results surpass what they initially hoped to achieve.

> *People have immeasurable potential that goes beyond what anyone may think they can achieve. If you can envision a goal, there is a good chance you can do even better; you just don't realize it yet. That's why you may feel surprised when you meet your stretch goals, going beyond what you perceived as your limit.*

We all could benefit from taking a look at ourselves beyond what we have been able to achieve to date. Each individual should aim for what he or she can achieve based on potential, not just performance so far, and pursue it with fanatical determination.

In other words, when viral leaders set goals, they ought to aim high and for the stars. That is why in this book, we encourage viral leaders to adopt the motto "Aim beyond!" Whatever your goals, we assume that you can reach them and go beyond your own expectations.

Another critical factor to consider is that if we want to constantly improve performance, we need to fully engage in the discipline of lifelong learning. Viral leadership is not a goal; it is a journey, always changing and evolving into something incrementally more exciting and productive.

ACTIVITY

With the concept "aim beyond!" in mind, take a moment to write down your goals for your role as a viral leader. What does the ideal *you* look like in that role? Remember: think big, and aim beyond! Don't settle for your level of past performance or the performance of others. Think of the ideal. Next, answer these questions:

- Which of your ideal characteristics do you already have?
- Which ones do you still need to develop?

Write down your answers and save them for later. You can use this template to help you. We encourage you to revisit your thoughts later and finetune them as we go along.

Description of the ideal viral leader.	What ideal characteristics do you already have?	What ideal characteristics do you still need to develop?

EXAMPLE

Description of the ideal viral leader.	What ideal characteristics do you already have?	What ideal characteristics do you still need to develop?
Great teacher, coach, and mentor *Manages difficult people effectively*	*Enjoy coaching one-on-one*	*Need practice presenting in front of large groups* *Need to learn to manage conflict*

Now, go viral. You can share this activity with your teams to help them aim beyond their current expectation of performance for themselves.

OVERCOMING SUCCESS SUPPRESSORS

> *Pessimism and optimism are slammed up against each other in my records. The tension between them is where it's all at. It's what lights the fire.*
> —BRUCE SPRINGSTEEN

SUPPRESSORS OF POTENTIAL

Despite our infinite potential, we face a chronic problem. Our potential can be dampened or suppressed by factors like fear, procrastination, confusion, and overall lack of motivation. These suppressors of potential have a dual impact.

First, they keep people from believing they can go beyond what they perceive they can achieve, which keeps them from realizing their true potential.

Second, because people believe in their perceived limitations, individuals and their teams fail to excel at work. In fact, they may even set goals below their limits to play it safe.

Perhaps the most critical problem is that suppressors of potential can be contagious. If we allow them to rule our lives, they become toxins that destroy the relationships we have worked so hard to develop. If we allow these toxins to spread, both our teams and our customers will suffer the consequences of poor management and leadership.

Let's take a closer look at some key suppressors. For a suppressor to be effective against our productivity, it has to be able to shake our confidence. After asking hundreds of leaders and managers about what makes them less confident, less assertive, and less productive at work, we've determined which suppressors are the most powerful.

SUPPRESSOR ONE: FEAR OR LACK OF CONFIDENCE

Fear comes in many shapes. For example, think of situations at work when you experienced a lack of confidence or when you felt less assertive. We don't always think of these feelings as fear, but you can see that they can be ways to react to fear.

When we experience fear, we react in a variety of predetermined ways often described as the fight-or-flight syndrome (also described as freeze, fight, or flight). Let's explore these responses.

When we feel uncomfortable, we may choose to do nothing and keep a low profile. This is a way to freeze, or hide from potential problems. Another manifestation of this response is looking away or pretending a problem isn't really there.

We might also consider flight in the form of avoiding the issue or the people causing us discomfort. When this happens, we try to create distance between ourselves and the issue. This distance may be physical, as in walking away, as well as metaphorical, as in claiming no role in what is taking place.

Finally, we might instead choose to fight. Unfortunately, when we do that from a stance of fear, our fight response displays in inappropriate ways, such as arguments and verbal disputes, which can even escalate into physical fights and altercations. In the worst cases, these reactions can lead to violence and death.

All of these responses lead to poor decisions, decreased productivity, rifts between teams and team members, lack of engagement, and overall dissatisfaction with our jobs. This is hardly the kind of viral leadership we hope to nurture.

SELF-CHECK

Think about the last time you felt fear or lack of confidence, or when you did not feel assertive. How did you react? What led you to react in that way? What are your sources of fear and lack of confidence and assertiveness? What keeps you from being decisive? Write these thoughts down, and we'll address them later when we explore how to maximize our strengths.

Being assertive does not always mean standing your ground or taking a stance. Sometimes, it involves being innovative in our approaches. There are many ways to achieve the same results; we just need to find the ways that best suit the situations and the people in them.

Going to the supervisor to demand an explanation of why he or she approved something might be perceived as challenging, and the supervisor could feel the need to be assertive about it. On the other hand, we can use less threatening ways to engage in discussion, such as asking our supervisor to help us learn via a coaching session or asking him or her to explain the rationale behind a recent decision so we can learn from it.

Sometimes we need to remember that while we have our own goals, we need to consider the other person first. If we know what someone's interests and goals are, we can tailor ours to align with them, and this can help us get what we want.

SUPPRESSOR TWO: PROCRASTINATION

The desire to leave tasks for the last minute can arise from a combination of factors, including poor time management and personal preferences. In some cases, procrastination can lead to anxiety, which then turns into fear, which in turn leads to lack of action and further procrastination.

Another behavior with effects similar to procrastination is the pursuit of perfection. Some people are paralyzed by the desire for perfection. They want to check with everyone and look at every possible angle to try to make everything absolutely perfect.

What is wrong with pursuing perfection? Isn't diligence a good thing? What makes this behavior unhealthy is taking it to the extreme. It is impossible to achieve perfection in an imperfect world. There is always something we can improve on, but if we keep chasing after perfection, we will never accomplish the task at hand.

One of the many challenges with procrastination is that it allows work and deadlines to pile up, making tasks harder to achieve. When we don't see a way out, we give up and let things run their course. These behaviors and attitudes can be demoralizing not only for the individual who has them but also for the people around them.

SELF-CHECK

Do you tend to leave the toughest tasks for last? Do you tend not to finish tasks on time? Is the pursuit of perfection your worst enemy?

The reasons for procrastination are many. Here are some of the most common:

Lack of engagement. Some people feel that their current tasks aren't interesting or valuable enough to pursue. This, at the most basic level, is a lack of motivation. We will address this later in the book.

Personality. The Myers-Briggs Type Instrument® (MBTI) is often used to detect an individual's preferences in how to process information, make decisions, and interact with and perceive the world.

The MBTI is an assessment that profiles preferences along four dimensions that describe our approaches to different aspects of our lives. For example, one dimension describes us as either judging (J) or perceiving (P). Those with a perceiving preference tend to make decisions at a slower pace than those with a judging preference. This is in part because Ps like to explore as many options as possible before reaching conclusions. Awareness of your own preferences might help you monitor and reduce your tendency to procrastinate.

SUPPRESSOR THREE: CONFUSION

Confusion or lack of clarity can also suppress action. Lack of clarity during goal setting has been identified as one of the top reasons for poor performance. As is the case with procrastination, confusion can lead to fear, which then leads to lack of action and further confusion.

A source of confusion is unclear (or no) priorities. We live in a world where the words "important," "urgent," "critical," and "necessary" are applied to nearly every assignment. When everything is a priority, nothing is. As a result, confusion ensues, and we end up with no action.

SELF-CHECK

Do you find it difficult to convey what you want to your teams and peers? Do you find that others struggle to follow your directions? We'll devote significant attention to the building of exceptional communication skills.

SUPPRESSOR FOUR: OVERALL LACK OF MOTIVATION

Overall lack of motivation comes in many forms—sometimes as deflection or blame. For example, some people choose not to perform a task if they perceive that their teammates are not pulling their weight, while other individuals might feel there is no significant reward for them upon completion of a task. There are also those who simply can't see how a task can be achieved. This hopelessness leads to an expectation of failure, and at this point, motivation drops to its lowest possible level.

SELF-CHECK

Is it hard for you to find intrinsic motivation? Do you often fail to see the value in what you do?

What makes you feel motivated to accomplish something? Think back to a time when you felt fully motivated by a leader. What did he or she do that you found most motivating?

RECAP

Let's review what we have discussed so far. Like in any journey, many conditions can make getting to our destination easier or harder. Imagine programming a trip on a navigation device. You may find a route that has delays and detours, or you may also find a better, more optimal route.

Like delays on a road, suppressors may slow us down or even stop us from making progress. But the ideal qualities of leaders and managers can help us to stay on track along the way and reach our goals.

When you think about the people who have been your role models and who have motivated you the most, which characteristics have made the greatest impact on you? Which of their traits helped you reach your goals? What made them viral leaders?

For most of us, the qualities that we look for in a motivational viral leader are character qualities that determine how they interact with us. This fact is at odds with what we normally think of when we ask, "What motivates an employee?" We are often led to think that financial rewards are what motivate people the most; however, when we go back to our own experiences, we often realize that money is not always what has motivated and inspired us.

What we learn from these observations is that if we want to become like these ideal leaders and managers, we cannot ignore the importance of refining our core skills in communication and relationship building.

We also learn that great leaders and managers don't just let us grow at our own pace. They actually motivate us to move at a pace a little faster than we are used to and sometimes even faster than we think possible. They change our expectations, encourage us to set a higher standard for ourselves, and help us discover qualities we didn't know we had or help us reach levels of performance that we didn't think we could achieve.

CHAPTER 5

VIRAL MOTIVATION—LEADING TEAMS TO TOP ACHIEVEMENT

The self-admirer, generally, should not glorify himself nor be so conceited that he elevates himself above his counterparts. Neither should he belittle himself to such an extent that he becomes inferior to his own peers or to those who are inferior both to him and to his fellowmen in the eyes of others. If he follows this advice, he will be freed from self-admiration and feelings of inferiority, and people will call him one who truly knows himself.
—MUHAMMAD IBN ZAKARIYA AL-RAZI

In the first half of 2014, Learning4Managers.com surveyed leaders from government and corporate fields to understand what factors make staff assertive, confident, and overall more productive. Our belief is that attitude and performance go hand in hand. Gaining a clear understanding of the key ingredients that affect our attitudes at work can provide us insight into what may help improve or affect work performance.

Confidence, assertiveness, and productivity are the qualities viral leaders use to infect their teams and motivate them to rise to the next level. The better we understand these qualities, the more we'll be able to take them viral.

The survey provides us with a first glance at what leaders perceive to affect assertive behaviors, confidence, and motivation. This first glance will allow us to further study and inquire about more specific work-performance enhancers and suppressors.

Most participants were from the United States, although there were no significant differences between the US responses and their counterparts from other countries. The survey questions were open ended, allowing participants to elaborate as much as they felt was needed. The survey asked about:

- Situations that made respondents less confident at work
- What factors decreased their productivity
- Specific examples of how managers motivated them

The job titles of the respondents fell into three main categories: C-level, such as chief executive officer or chief financial officer (21 percent), vice president or director level (42 percent), and manager (37 percent). Most of the participants came from the corporate world (68 percent of respondents), while the rest were evenly divided at 16 percent between education (e.g., academic institutions such as universities) and government.

ASSERTIVENESS AT WORK

One of the major determinants of effectiveness at work is assertiveness, which includes refusal to be intimidated by others. Lack of assertiveness is known to lead to issues such as bullying in the workplace.

A survey on bullying at 516 private and public organizations conducted by the National Institute for Occupational Safety and Health (NIOSH) indicates the following:

- Of the companies surveyed, 24.5 percent reported that some degree of bullying had occurred during the preceding year.
- In the most recent incidents, 39.2 percent involved an employee as the aggressor, 24.5 percent involved a customer, and 14.7 percent involved a supervisor.
- In the most recent incidents, 55.2 percent involved the employee as the victim, 10.5 percent involved the customer, and 7.7 percent involved the supervisor.

Bullying was defined as repeated intimidation, slandering, social isolation, or humiliation by one or more persons against another.

The 2014 Learning4Managers survey gathered initial views on what makes people feel assertive at work and what keeps them from being so.

JOB TITLE

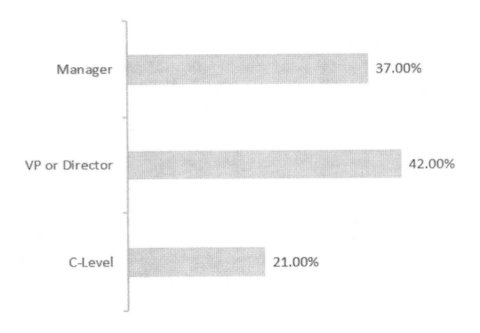

INDUSTRY

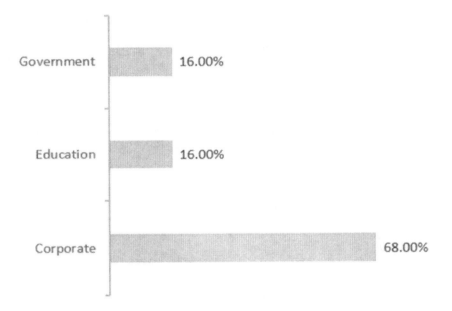

THE FINDINGS: ASSERTIVE BEHAVIOR

Responses to this question indicated that the more people know about the situation or subject matter they're handling, the more assertive they feel about what they are doing and planning to do.

The next most common factor that affects assertiveness is perceiving a need or pressure to do a task. An impending deadline or awareness that the task is important enough to merit completion, for example, makes people assertive about moving forward with plans and completing tasks.

The third highest number of responses indicated that assertiveness is also driven by passion. If someone cares strongly about a task, he or she feels more assertive and motivated to complete it.

The survey also indicated that what makes us feel less assertive falls into three categories. The first is collaboration. When there is strong teamwork, there is less need to be assertive, as things move ahead naturally. On the other hand, when there is conflict or if people perceive the potential for loss, they may become less assertive. Finally, lack of pressure, whether due to low motivation or incentive (positive or negative), decreases the need to be assertive.

THE FINDINGS: CONFIDENCE

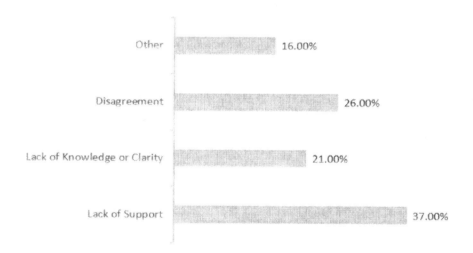

Our survey revealed that when people feel they do not receive sufficient support from their managers or peers, they lose confidence. Some of the lack of support is attributed to the workplace culture. If it isn't nurturing and promotes intimidation, distrust, and lack of cohesion, confidence suffers.

Next, the survey showed that the lack of clear instructions and expectations or clarity on what the approach should be can lead to lack of confidence.

When there are no clear goals, instructions, or training, people lose confidence in their ability to perform well.

Finally, about 26 percent of respondents indicated that they lost confidence when they perceived strong disagreement from a person they consulted for an expert opinion. Specifically, people perceive a loss of self-confidence when someone in authority disagrees with their opinion, resulting in conflict.

THE FINDINGS: PRODUCTIVITY

We were able to identify four clear categories of what makes people less productive.

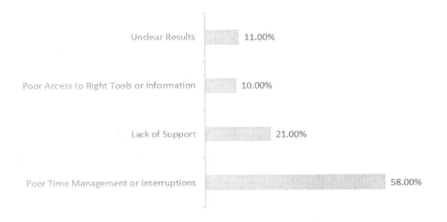

Time management: Time-management issues, including interruptions, were at the top of the list. Other time-management issues included frequent meetings, lack of relevant content in meetings, and poor managerial guidance regarding time allocation for projects. Wait time was also mentioned, as in waiting for other employees, vendors, machines, or customers to complete their tasks before the survey respondent was able to move ahead with their own. Examples of wait time include having to wait for supplies to be delivered or waiting for an e-mail confirmation from a customer.

Lack of support: Lack of team and managerial support came next. Micromanagement, lack of recognition, and lack of trust in employees appeared to be common issues too. Distrust and lack of team cohesion were also mentioned as common issues.

Unclear expectations: Participants mentioned their frustration and loss of productivity when desired results and goals were unclear and when leaders failed to provide direction or feedback on a proposed approach.

Limited access to tools or information: Finally, the last category involved poor or lack of access to the right tools and information to accomplish the task at hand.

THE FINDINGS: MOTIVATORS

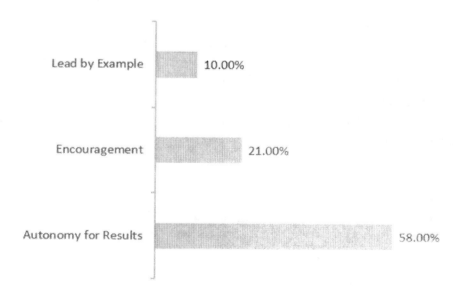

At the top of the list of what motivates survey respondents (48 percent) is encouragement. Encouragement and recognition from both peers and managers motivates them to perform better.

Being given autonomy in pursuit of results is also one of the top three motivators for performance, with 26 percent of responses.

Another 26 percent indicated that leading by example was perceived as the greatest motivator.

PRACTICAL FINDINGS VIRAL LEADERS CAN USE
Let's review each of the key factors the survey found that impact productivity and results the most.

KNOWLEDGE
Knowledge and expertise allow us to feel assertive and confident. This is backed by other research. People are most engaged when they believe they know and understand their jobs. Viral leaders often capitalize on this fact.

Managers should consider that without adequate knowledge, employees are prone to act tentatively and with less confidence. This observation clearly stresses the importance of training and shows that managers need to explain team and individual goals and instructions clearly, seeking regular feedback from staff regarding how well they understand tasks and assignments and whether they have what they need to complete them. We recommend that managers consider taking "train-the-trainer" courses and training on how to give effective presentations.

For individuals, the findings indicate that all employees need to take the responsibility of asking for more information when needed. Employees need to ask for competency-building opportunities and training for acting assertively and with confidence. Individuals may benefit from communication-skills training to learn how to communicate their needs better.

PRESSURE

There appear to be two kinds of pressure discussed in the survey responses. There is negative pressure or distress and the threat of negative consequences, but there is also positive pressure, or eustress. Positive pressure and negative pressure lead to very different attitudes and behaviors.

Survey respondents pointed out how negative pressure (e.g., unrealistic deadlines, negative attitudes at work, conflict) could make people less assertive, less confident, and less productive. Among the sources of negative pressure were unclear or unachievable expectations set by managers or clients.

Managers should consider taking a closer look at how they set goals and expectations. They should also consider the types of behaviors and attitudes that can lead to negative stress and train people on how to manage them. Suggested training topics include personality types, managing team interactions, managing differences of opinion, and managing conflict.

Positive pressure, the kind of pressure we see in some competitive people, appears to be motivating and rewarding. Managers should consider what kind of work environment encourages this kind of pressure. Staff members with clear visions of their goals tend to feel this sort of positive pressure. To improve in this area, managers might benefit from strategy and goal-development training.

SUPPORT AND PASSION LEAD TO PRODUCTIVITY

The best levels of assertiveness, confidence, and productivity seem to be achieved when people feel passionate about what they do. This state of passion can exist only if people feel the support they need from their managers and their teams.

Based on the survey responses, people found certain managerial behaviors supportive: giving employees recognition, offering clear goals and instructions, providing the right training for the job so they know exactly what to do and how to do it, listening to them, and responding to their needs. These behaviors are clear indications of great viral leaders.

Being a viral leader also includes showing trust in employees' abilities and expertise and avoiding behaviors that may be perceived as micromanagement. People appear to expect a balance between reasonable amounts of autonomy without feeling abandoned and hands-on management. Leading by example also appears to be a strong motivator for higher performance.

Our experience with team and management interactions leads us to conclude that teams seeking to find this level of passion at work can benefit from understanding how different personalities interact with each other. Learning how each type of personality prefers to communicate and approach different tasks can help build a stronger sense of support and unity. Viral leaders can teach teams how to leverage the strengths of each member to achieve better results.

WHAT TO ELIMINATE

A final observation is that there are elements that workplaces should eliminate. Time wasters are some of the most obvious, leading to a decrease in performance and confidence according to the survey.

The most common time wasters mentioned in the survey were interruptions, which include e-mail, phone calls, unnecessary meetings, and so forth. These issues may be best addressed by providing teams and individuals adequate time-management training as well as effective meeting-management training.

Other causes of wasted time are wait time, often when one person depends on another person or department to complete a task before he or she can move ahead on something. Other instances of wasted time can be attributed to poor planning. These responses indicate a need for project-management training and strategy-planning training.

Participate in the survey! Follow this link: **http://viralleaders.com/?p=43**

SUMMARY OF CHALLENGES

Based on our observations and the survey results, we have identified these as the top three challenges for managers and leaders today:

Lack of Clarity. When expectations are not clear and when people are confused about how to do their jobs, individuals tend to act in ways that are nonproductive. Poor communication contributes to waste and often creates tensions that lead to the next challenge: conflict.

Conflict. Tensions can grow and become barriers to progress. As conflict develops, communication becomes more difficult, which contributes to continued lack of clarity. More resources are allocated to managing conflict and less to getting tasks done, which leads to the final challenge: waste.

Waste. From distractions to poor resource utilization, waste can lead to stress, which in turn contributes to conflict and lack of clarity.

Lack of Clarity → Confusion → Conflict → Waste

All three challenges, if left unchecked, work together to energize each other and conspire to defeat even the most effective teams. Great leaders and managers understand these three critical obstacles and the need to overcome them to help their teams reach higher levels of performance.

To address these obstacles, we'll focus on the mechanics of how we think and how these thinking processes can help us tailor motivational strategies and interventions that fit each individual.

ELICITING OPTIMAL PERFORMANCE—VIRALITY

Many managers struggle with employee performance. This is evident when you look at job descriptions, which often list "self-starters" or "independent thinkers" and other similar qualities as highly desired characteristics.

The fact is that at work, you'll find different kinds of individuals. There are those who need prompts to do their jobs as well as those who are self-motivated to perform their job functions and even those who look for additional duties beyond their own.

Many leaders hope for the last type to work for them, because they believe that these individuals will work with as little supervision as possible. How could that be a bad thing, after all? They also hope to avoid those who appear to need direction, because they appear to be the least motivated individuals in the group.

The issues leaders face with highly motivated people are not as obvious as those you'd expect with low-motivated individuals. The trouble begins when these highly independent and self-motivated people divert their attention to extracurricular activities at work that are not aligned with the corporate objectives. For example, a motivated employee at a retail clothing store may feel the urge to survey customers on their color preferences for the season and report back to the manager; however, the manager may not feel this is appropriate to that employee's responsibilities.

High energy and motivation can be assets, but only when they are pointed in the right direction. Don't assume that just because someone shows initiative, he or she automatically knows what to do or where there are boundaries not to cross. Always set clear expectations with individuals and discuss clearly what the boundaries are, both in terms of minimum expectations as well as how far their independence can reach.

Exemplary leaders and managers, those people we call viral leaders, look at the individual as a whole. They appeal to the individual's heart and mind to provoke action. This is one of the keys of successful leadership and management. Without engaging the muscle, without being able to motivate people to act, leaders and managers are ineffective.

Even the most inspiring message is useless if it fails to instigate action of some sort. That is why for leaders to become viral, they need to develop that quality that allows them to infect others with the passion to take action. We call this quality "virality," and it is the ultimate proof of a viral leader.

What do great leaders and managers do to get people to act? How do they become viral? They start by gaining an understanding of how people think and how they make decisions. For some, this is a natural skill, while for others, it is learned. Knowing what motivates individuals to make the decisions they make helps them become powers of influence.

MOTIVATED PEOPLE

Research studies tell us that motivation is the result of two components: value and the expectation of success. The first component helps us determine if a task is worth doing, while the second is based on our best estimate of whether we can succeed. This is what we call the "motivation equation."

THE MOTIVATION EQUATION

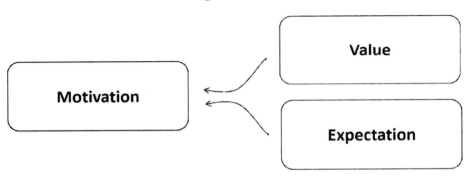

Let's consider the implications of the motivation equation for a moment. If we believe we can achieve a goal and that the goal is of value to us, then we become interested in pursuing it. The more value we attribute to the goal and the easier it is to attain, the more motivated we feel.

Another way to understand this concept is by looking at it from the reverse side. How motivated are you to do a task if you know you are guaranteed to fail?

Motivated people perceive value in what they are about to do and how soon they expect to succeed. People expect a reward of sorts for the effort they put into doing something. And the sooner they expect the reward to come, the better for motivation.

Educators, psychologists, and marketing experts have known this for a long time. Teachers know that once a student leaves school for home, education competes with all kinds of media for that student's attention. So if teachers want to encourage students to do their homework and do it with motivation, the assignments need to capture students' attention. These assignments have to be interesting and feel valuable to the students. If they aren't, students may forget to do the homework completely or else do just enough to get it over with and move on to something they prefer. In this case, the value is associated not with the assignment but with something else.

Let's see how psychologists apply the idea of perceived value. Just turn on any TV show featuring a doctor discussing someone's poor health habits. The audience can't understand why the person continues to do something that he or she knows is detrimental for him or her and those around him or her. Soon you hear a psychologist on the show (who is sometimes the host), ask the person, "What do you get out of acting like this? What is the reward?"

Psychologists understand that motives behind behaviors are based on expectations of reward because of past experience. That is why, when trying to correct a behavior, they ask someone to state what he or she would rather do instead of continuing his or her current behavior. Psychologists then ask, "And what would that change be worth to you?" They hope to help the person rethink what he or she values most—the reward from the bad behavior or the reward from correcting it.

Then the TV show uses perceived-value psychology on you, the viewer. To know how the person on the show answers, you must watch a commercial created by the finest marketing and advertising experts. They get your attention with something you value. Do you want a perfect body? Do you want lots of friends? Do you want to have it all with little effort? They do their best to engage you by touching what they know motivates you—by presenting to you what you value—and by making it look easy to get.

To motivate people to become high performers, viral leaders focus on building value and setting the right expectations behind each goal they want their teams to meet.

THE QUESTION OF VALUE

As we've seen, part of the motivation equation is value. A person's willingness and motivation to learn is influenced greatly by the value that person places on the knowledge to be gained. We know that someone is more likely to attend a course or a seminar about a subject he or she finds valuable.

To understand how people determine value, we can look into what we know from sales and marketing research. An individual decides on the value of something based on his or her perception of quality, relevance, and on how accessible or available it is.

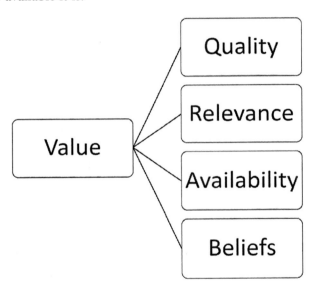

AVAILABILITY

Marketers position a product as a limited-edition item because they know that people perceive a higher value in what only a few people can have. Scarcity—when there is not enough of something for which there is a perceived need or a perceived high value—can drive demand through the roof.

QUALITY

Quality is most often determined by reliability. For example, if you watch a movie directed and produced by someone well known for these skills, you expect similar quality to what you have seen before from the same person.

If a manufacturer has been known to lie about the reliability of a product, then you will perceive the item as of poor quality even before you use it. If the item is produced by a brand you trust, you perceive it as valuable and dismiss low-reliability products by that brand as exceptions.

People also perceive quality by association. Let's say that an e-learning course's technology fails. The course itself could be considered less reliable and therefore of lower quality. Likewise, if the binding for a manual falls apart, it could cause people to question its overall quality, including the quality of the content.

RELEVANCE

A person measures relevance by what he or she finds interesting and applicable to meet a need. Relevance also includes components of timeliness and urgency. The more immediate or urgent the need, the higher the relevance.

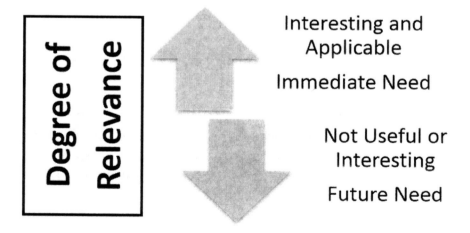

BELIEFS

The final element of value assessment is our belief and value systems. We place value on those objects that our belief and value systems tell us are important. While a strong belief system may appear to be a positive thing, one negative aspect of a belief system is that it has the potential to create and nurture biases.

We may create biases in our minds in favor or against certain people or brands or even products. Our biases may blind us and rob us of opportunities, because they change our perspective on their true value.

Now, let's explore value from the perspective of viral leadership. Traditional leaders rely on annual performance reviews to motivate employees. Performance reviews are often tied to bonuses, which traditional leaders hope will impact performance.

But talk to managers and employees and ask them how they feel about conducting annual reviews. While a few may feel they are great experiences, most state that reviews are a waste of time. In fact, most managers do not work on performance-review paperwork until the last minute, and complete the process not because they see value in it but because they see value in meeting the deadline.

Team members often think that review time is when they should fight for their bonuses, but do not see a direct relationship between the judgments in the review and their actual performance. There is a clear disconnect between performance reviews and their intent.

To motivate performance, viral leaders make sure that each team member understands how valuable his or her work is to the organization and to those around him or her. When the team member sees value in what he or she does and how this value extends to others, the team member's motivation rises.

Viral leaders also regularly review any tasks that a team member does not find valuable to help him or her gain a better perspective. Perhaps a team member does not see the importance of the task—or perhaps the leader has not realized that the task is indeed of little value and needs to be removed or changed to render it valuable.

When trying to motivate someone to complete a task or meet a goal, viral leaders ask themselves how each team member perceives its value:

- Is this a task worth his or her time and effort?
- How can this goal or task help reflect the quality of this team member once achieved?
- Is this task timely and relevant to the circumstances now?
- Is there any uniqueness to this task?

Picture a manager preparing to tell the team at a warehouse that it is time to take inventory of small parts. This is a menial task, usually boring, and, in the eyes of many employees, useless. Many wonder, "Who cares about a missing bolt or two here and there? The company makes enough money not to worry about a few missing parts. Plus, the cost of paying people to do inventory is probably much higher than what might be missing." Another member thinks, "It sounds like the company doesn't trust us again and is now checking to make sure we didn't steal a stupid box of screws." If the value isn't perceived, motivation falters. But what if the value is not in the task itself but in the experience?

A viral leader meets with the team to see how to make the experience valuable for everyone. After a few discussions, the leader announces that inventory time is near, but this time, it will be a great, fun party with plenty of breaks, food, and music. People will work in teams, and there will be hourly prizes for teams completing tasks quickly and accurately.

At the end of the inventory task, the managers provide an overview of what was accomplished that day and what items might be missing and impact upcoming needs. They point out that an accurate count of parts improves everyone's ability to do their jobs well—and they recognize those who do.

By identifying what is valuable to that team and creating an opportunity for team-building activities, have a relaxing day, and have the team be truly heard by the managers, these viral leaders turn the task into a valuable and motivating one.

EXPECTATION AFFECTS MOTIVATION

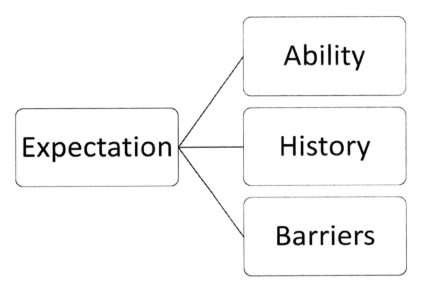

Imagine a marketing manager discussing a marketing plan for a new product with her peer. As they try to determine what segment of their customer base to target first, the more experienced marketer of the two says, "Let's go for the low-hanging fruit." By that, of course, she means the easiest to reach. This one phrase illustrates the nature of human motivation.

BARRIERS

People are motivated by low-hanging fruit. The beauty of low-hanging fruit is that we know that if we simply reach out for it, the probability of our success is very high. With no barriers between us and the fruit, we are almost guaranteed to reach it with minimum effort in a relatively short time. This makes low-hanging fruit more desirable than the fruit at the top of the tree.

Not all barriers are physical. Sometimes we may not feel as motivated to do something when there are emotional or psychological barriers. Our fears of the unknown and of failure may become barriers we may not feel able to overcome.

HISTORY
We often go back to our own experiences to determine whether something is possible. If the past tells us that a certain task is not easily achievable or may even be impossible, we probably won't expect to achieve it.

ABILITY
Ability is tied to skill and performance. If people perceive that they have the skills to achieve a goal, they may feel more motivated than if they believe they lack the skills. Without the skills to do something, their expectation of success may be much lower, which in turn reduces motivation.

APPLYING THE FORMULA
Now that we understand the motivation equation, let's take a look at how it applies in the day-to-day activities of emerging and experienced viral leaders.

Working our way back from the end of the formula, let's begin with expectation. As we discussed earlier, lack of clarity can have a negative impact on our perspectives and diminish our expectations of success. To remove suppressors and to support our expectations of success, we can use an often-underestimated tool: SWOT analysis (and its companion, min-max review). This tool is described in detail in the second part of this book.

This analysis tool will help you and your team identify your *strengths, weaknesses, opportunities,* and *threats* (SWOT). One reason that leaders fail is because they try to focus on their own weaknesses and those of their teams. They work hard at trying to strengthen these weaknesses, thinking that only then will they become stronger.

Consider this example: Of two athletes, one is a medal-winning sprinter and long-distance runner. The other has won medals by lifting the heaviest of weights. Their strengths are obvious. But let's force them to switch places and tell them we expect them to win medals in their new fields. What do you think will happen?

A viral leader helps team members clarify and understand their strengths and how they can use them to meet specific goals. Placing the focus on weaknesses only frustrates everyone and yields a minimal reward as a result.

The real value of the SWOT analysis is in the min-max review. In this review, you assess where the greatest potential for success truly is. When people see their abilities aligned with their previous performance or history of success and can visualize a way past the barriers, their expectation for success can increase.

It also helps you identify where you can avoid wasting resources and time. By identifying weaknesses and their matching threats, you'll quickly know what you want to stay away from. To try to build a case from a position of weakness, where the odds are against you, is simply a losing proposition.

To put it another way, min-max is a way of bringing the fruit at the top of the tree to the bottom and turning it into the proverbial low-hanging fruit. Once you help your team members gain clarity regarding where their strengths are and match them to opportunity, then your team will have clarity of expectation.

Next, we need to address value. Viral leaders understand that people always ask, silently or out loud, "What is in it for me?" Viral leaders answer this question by helping people find value in what they are being asked to do.

Once again, the min-max review of your SWOT analysis will help you uncover and challenge potential negative biases and replace them with more constructive and positive beliefs. You will also focus on opportunities, which means you'll identify both availability and relevance in the task at hand.

Finally, you can address the issue of quality by matching each team member's strengths with the opportunity before him or her. You are giving your team members the chance to shine as they rise to their tasks. If you can help your team members find all these qualities in the tasks you ask of them, you'll have established value.

With expectation (this is low-hanging fruit) and value (what's in it for me?) addressed, you are now a viral leader. You have passed on the motivation needed to ignite action, and you are ready to take your team to the next level of performance.

ASSEMBLING THE RIGHT TEAMS

Selecting the right candidates to work with makes it easier for all team members to be more productive. Viral leaders should choose the right team members as early as possible.

When selecting candidates for a job—whether in hiring, assigning the lead role on a project, or staffing a special team—we need to watch out for communication traps. Sometimes these traps come from biases we have created about people, which can lead us to give the wrong signals. We may select those whose communication styles we prefer. We may also ignore the communication styles of others, and in doing so, we may put questions in ways that make it difficult for a candidate to understand us or to answer fully.

Other times, the traps may come with the candidate. We may not recognize cultural biases or communication styles that are not obvious to us but make us read a candidate as too strong or too weak. If you work with remote teams in other parts of the world or with a team of individuals from a variety of countries, cross-cultural and language issues may arise in performance reviews, which may add to the confusion and complexity of the matter.

Ultimately, we want to hire or select the person best suited for the job or the person who can actually do the job. However, we don't always have the luxury of seeing the person in action. In most selection processes, we are forced to rely on the interview process and a few conversations to make our choices. Here is where effective communication from both sides of the table comes into play.

Our next challenge is to ensure that we hire for skill, not personality. Communication styles can distract us from our objectives and lead us down the path of stereotyping.

Professionals from a large variety of fields have shared with us several examples of situations where communication style rather than the candidate's skills themselves can affect the outcome of an interview. For instance, some candidates seem too descriptive if the interviewers prefer to hear the bottom line.

Some examples identified corporate stereotypes and showed how even our visual communication (how we look) can impact an interview.

Experience teaches us many lessons. In the world of interviewing, it becomes critical for us to grow, learn, and practice communication skills and for us to learn about our own strengths and growth areas. Our best bet is to stay focused on the specifics of the job and come prepared in our process for selecting candidates.

CHAPTER 6

SUSTAINING LEADERSHIP VIRALITY

An old Cherokee found his grandson fighting with another young boy
who had offended him. The grandfather decided to teach his grandson
an important lesson. So they sat together as the old man told the story
of the two wolves. "A terrible fight goes on inside me every day," he
told the young boy. "It is a difficult fight, and it is a fight between
two wolves. One of the wolves is evil and quick to anger. All he knows
is hate, envy, greed, arrogance, and lies. The other wolf is good and
seeks only justice. All he knows is truth, peace, love, humility, and
kindness. The same fight is going on inside you now, and inside me,
and inside everyone you see here around us," the old man said.
The grandson thought about his grandfather's words
and then asked, "Which wolf wins?"

The old man smiled and said, "The one you feed."
—"The Two Wolves," a Cherokee legend

Our next challenge will be to keep the motivation and the action going. It is one thing to start off well. It is another to maintain that initial momentum. In this section, we'll address how to make viral leadership sustainable over the long term.

Many cultures share similar stories to the Cherokee legend of the two wolves about the two sides of human nature. In the Western world, for example, we often picture an individual with a small angel and a small devil sitting on either shoulder and trying to influence that person's behavior.

What these stories and images tell us is that our decisions and behaviors are influenced not just by our surroundings but by different forces within us. Scientific discoveries about the brain and behavior are helping us understand these influences, and they may also hold the key to helping us understand ourselves better.

Let's use this knowledge to focus our effort on understanding people, the decisions they make, and the reasons they act the way they do. This knowledge will help us know where to direct our efforts when we try to influence others.

The ability to influence customers and employees is a necessary skill for many. However, it appears that some are far better at it than others. What are they doing differently, and what can we do to be more like them?

To get better results, researchers suggest that you should pay closer attention to two very important factors: your mirroring skills and your attitude toward the product or the service you offer. For example, research conducted by Duke University in 2007 shows that mirroring the customer's behavior can influence his or her decision to buy. The study revealed that by making a conscious effort to mimic the customer and showing interest in your offering, you can increase your chances of closing the sale. Similar studies by Université de Bretagne–Sud indicate that mirroring can, in some cases, influence people enough to increase sales by up to 17 percent.

Mirroring is something many successful sales people do intuitively. However, what's interesting in the Duke report is that demonstrating a positive attitude and enthusiasm about your product or service can further increase your sales ratios.

The important lesson we can take away from these studies is that nothing influences others more than your own attitudes and behaviors. Pay attention to the other person's use of language and body language and start mirroring them. Furthermore, focus on your enthusiasm for the idea you are presenting to the other person. These steps will help you win them over.

To help you master these communication skills, we'll talk about the three-signal communication model. This model helps us gain a bird's-eye view of how the brain works to help us perceive our environments, interpret them, make decisions about how to interact with them, and, finally, take action.

The model may appear familiar to you if you have read the work of Paul D. MacLean on the triune brain, but in our model, we are not studying the biology of neuroscience. It is not our intent to give a biology lesson on the brain and how it functions; neither do we want to lecture on psychology and psychiatry. Our intent is rather to provide you with practical applications and strategies to enhance performance at work: we are only focusing on behavioral observations and how we arrive at decisions and actions.

Remember, too, that we intend to give you only a representation of the very complex world of human interactions and behaviors. The models we show you are not perfect reflections of reality. They just help us understand reality by means of simpler symbols.

THE THREE-SIGNAL COMMUNICATION MODEL

Earlier, we mentioned how viral leaders and managers pay attention to three areas in each individual: their hearts, their minds, and their muscles. In this section, we'll use a simple model to help us understand how we can reach out to each of these areas to influence people to perform at higher levels. The model provides a simplified view of how we think and why we act the way we do, which helps us understand why we become engaged in an activity or task.

Imagine a concert by three a cappella singers where each one holds a different microphone. Each microphone is controlled by a separate slider on a sound board. The Three-Signal Communication model is like a set of three sliders. Each one turns the volume or the intensity of three different internal voices up or down in our minds, as if each of them were using a different microphone. Let's explore these internal voices.

THE FIRST SIGNAL: BIOLOGICAL

All living creatures are designed to survive, and we all have biological mechanisms to help us do that. Our brain is programmed at the most primal level to keep us from harm. For example, our brains tell us to remove our hands when we put them near something that could burn us and to find cover in the middle of a storm.

Abraham Maslow describes this biological need in his 1943 paper "A Theory of Human Motivation," and his work is still validated in research today. He developed what we commonly know today as Maslow's hierarchy of needs. Maslow observed that at the most basic level, we are all about survival. In our model, we'll call this our biological signal.

When interacting with others, our biological signal reacts to anything it perceives as a threat. It could be a loud voice or aggressive body language—perhaps even the look on someone's face. If we sense any hint of danger or sense that we should not trust the other person, the biological signal takes over and tells us to respond accordingly to protect ourselves.

This instinctive reaction is what we sometimes call our "gut instinct." It is an internal alert that tells us to seek safety and to stay away from danger. We may not be able to explain it rationally, and sometimes we are not even fully consciously aware of its influence, but we often obey it above any other signal.

Of course, there is more to humans than just this basic level. We also make decisions based on our thoughts and our feelings. In fact, Carl Jung's work, expanded by the research around the Myers-Briggs Type Instrument® (MBTI), shows us that the way in which we make decisions is based on certain functions related to our feeling and thinking abilities.

THE SECOND SIGNAL: RELATIONAL

On the feelings side, we know we are relationship-driven beings and need to stay connected with others to build communities. Research shows that our brains have areas developed specifically for language, interaction with others, and relationships. Our ability to use language is an example of how we are driven to communicate beyond our basic needs to share emotions, feelings, and to stay connected to others. We'll call this our relational signal. Our internal relational signal focuses on the tone of our conversations and the word choices we make. It is the one that also listens for metamessages, those implied messages behind how things are said. The voice in our minds allows us to communicate empathy and genuineness when necessary.

This voice also helps us know our emotional state. The Institute of Neuroscience and Psychology at the University of Glasgow published recent research in the journal *Current Biology* about our emotions. They identified that humans display four primary emotions: happy, sad, afraid/surprised, and angry/disgusted. These emotions provide one more layer of interpretation to the messages we send and receive.

THE THIRD SIGNAL: LOGICAL

Finally, let's talk about our thinking side. We recognize that we have an ability to use reasoning and think logically. We usually depend on this voice to formulate strategies and imagine scenarios to predict outcomes. We'll call this the logical signal.

On the one hand, this voice can be very helpful in determining the pros and cons of a situation and in balancing our instincts and emotions. But when it takes over, it can make us seem uncaring and cold.

WORKING TOGETHER—WHAT SONG ARE THEY SINGING, AND WHO IS LEADING?

These three signals of our being are like the two wolves or the angels and devils on our shoulders. They influence how we think and how we behave. They help us survive, build relationships, and plan for the future. But as the legends and stories of old teach us, we need to learn to nurture the parts of us that are constructive and positive. Let's explore how we can do that.

We can think of a cappella singing as a metaphor for how we think and behave. When performing an a cappella song, the singers may sing as a chorus, or they may have a lead vocalist while the others provide background support. Our actions are often a mix of our biological, relational, and logical signals or voices working together to form a melody or, in this case, a decision. Sometimes, one voice is more intense than the rest, and sometimes one voice might be much less intense than the others. The mix of these three signals leads us to different tunes/decisions, each with its very own, unique blend.

Let's take a look at three simple examples:

- **Biological signal in the lead.** Hunger is an important primal need that directs us to eat so we can survive. But if we eat to excess, weight problems and eventually health issues can develop. Our logical voice helps us make better decisions and limit our food intake.
- **Relational signal in the lead.** Trust is a key tool in building relationships. But too much trust can make us naïve, while too little can turn us into hermits. Our biological voice helps us know through instinct when something is not right.
- **Logical signal in the lead.** Are you thinking of buying a car? If you wait for your logical voice to gather the details on all available vehicles to make the best possible decision, you might never buy anything. Our relational voice helps us limit our choices when we select something based on what others might think or what our family might need.

THE THREE-SIGNAL MODEL AND LEADERSHIP

As you can see, the first challenge we struggle with every day is finding the perfect balance among our three internal signals—biological, relational, and logical—to continue moving forward with our lives. That is why when we make decisions, our brain systems try to find the route to the best possible decisions in the shortest time possible.

Imagine if we allowed the three signals to keep debating over every decision we made daily. *Should I cross the street or wait here where it's safe? If I stay put, am I really safer? And what about the person waiting for me in the building across the street? Will he worry if I'm late?* If our brains didn't make quick decisions, it would be simply impractical.

Let's see the three signals in action. A manager welcomes a new member into a sales team. The new member is excited but also a little nervous. That same week, the new sales-team member has the misfortune of meeting a dissatisfied customer who demands a refund for a product he bought last year. The item is past warranty and cannot be refunded. Our salesperson tries to no avail to calm the customer, who now threatens to contact the manager. The salesperson can't convince the customer to change his mind. All the salesperson can do now is do the right thing: stick to policy and hope the manager will understand the situation.

The next day, the manager calls the sales-team member, saying a complaint came in and wanting to hear an explanation. The manager does not sound happy. What motivational signals do you think are at play now, and what level of intensity does each have in the mind of the new salesperson?

Let's take a look at the signals in the scenario:

- Biological: Fear is sending intense signals. The instinct for flight tells the salesperson to simply quit before getting fired. The threat has caused a lot of stress and is exerting a toll on the salesperson's body.
- Relational: This is a very emotional situation. The salesperson didn't want to disappoint the customer or the manager. The salesperson hopes that the manager will understand that the customer's demand was unreasonable.
- Logical: The salesperson knows that the customer's request was unreasonable. Keeping a cool head is important for explaining the issue to the manager. Quitting now would cause a whole new set of problems, so the salesperson feels it is better to calm down and explain what happened in a logical way.

Which signal will sound the loudest? Remember the two wolves? Whichever one gets fed has the most energy. Remember, the mind will be tempted to address the situation using the fastest route. This approach is quite limited and can lead to mistakes. However, as long as the risk is tolerable, we continue to make decisions the same way unless we make a conscious effort to analyze our responses.

What this means to us at work is that we need to look at our decisions and interactions through the lenses of the biological, relational, and logical signal perspectives. Furthermore, we need to understand the important role leaders play in decision making.

In our scenario, the salesperson is not the only one who can feed energy to his or her own signals. Energy can come from the leader too. The manager's approach of calling and demanding an explanation helped feed the insecurities of the biological and relational signals.

We fear the unknown, and we feel intimidated when we sense a loss of our power. We experience similar feelings when we are put in unfamiliar situations and when we feel powerless at work. We are not necessarily afraid, but we have similar feelings—which can make us feel less confident and less assertive. They can also lead to bad choices.

Let's take a closer look at how a viral leader can take advantage of all this information on signals. Let's revisit some communication basics.

COMMUNICATION-SKILLS BASICS

> *The single biggest problem in communication*
> *is the illusion that it has taken place.*
> —GEORGE BERNARD SHAW

As human beings, we want to build connections with others. It is part of who we are. To accomplish that, we use different means of communication. Conventional wisdom divides our communication into three areas: verbal, paraverbal, and nonverbal.

Verbal focuses on the content of what is being said. Verbal communication can be written or spoken. Our logical voice favors this communication component because it allows us to discuss descriptions, numbers, and data in general.

This does not mean our relational voice doesn't use verbal communication. On the contrary, many of our emotions are communicated with words.

Paraverbal focuses on the way the content is presented using tone, cadence, and speed of communication. A person may speak loudly or may type a word entirely in capital letters to get someone's attention. Another person may communicate in a softer way to convey a caring disposition.

In a letter or e-mail, paraverbal messages may be conveyed by using images, visual cues, or text formatting. Our relational voice takes advantage of this type of communication to interpret and communicate messages. The paraverbal component of communication helps us build or hinder relationships.

Nonverbal focuses on the way we communicate when we use our bodies and not words. This is the component of communication we are usually the least aware of. This is also the area most favored by our biological voice. You can easily tell when someone is startled by looking at the way his or her body reacts. The speed and manner in which we move and breathe and the expressions we use help us convey a significant portion of what we mean to share.

COMMUNICATION SKILLS AND THE THREE-SIGNAL MODEL

Let's explore how our different signals work with the different ways in which we communicate. Imagine you go overseas to an exotic island. The first night, at a restaurant, you order a local dish you have never heard of before. The waiter gets excited and tells you how much he loves your choice. Not only is the dish the waiter's favorite, it is also the house specialty.

When the dish arrives, you smell the food on the plate and immediately pull back while you put on your best "yuck" face. Your biological signal took charge before you had a chance to even think about what was happening.

The waiter does not need to hear you say the word "yuck" to know you don't like the smell of the dish. He can see it in your face. This nonverbal facial expression is universally identified as one of disgust. The reaction is part of your biological signal that helps you to protect yourself from eating food that could make you sick.

Now, you glance at the waiter and see how he reacts to your initial response. Your relational signal speaks up, and you begin to feel bad for him. The more you think about it, you realize that you might have even offended him by your reaction. So, as the waiter rushes to take the plate away, you ask him not to. You use a very soft and caring tone. This is your relational signal influencing your decisions and trying to find harmony. You decide you don't want to offend the waiter and pretend to hide your initial disgust.

You eat the dish, and the waiter comes by one more time to ask if you would like some dessert. You would love to try something that would get rid of the taste in your mouth, but now you are more cautious. You realize that you don't know any of the desserts on the menu, and now you wonder if they will all taste awful. So you tell the waiter you are too full for dessert and that you are ready to pay the bill. You state your request for the bill in a simple, matter-of-fact sort of way. This is your logical signal influencing your thinking and helping you strategize and plan ahead.

As you can see, what we say and the ways in which we convey our messages can give us a glimpse of how our brain might be working in certain scenarios. If we listen carefully and pay attention to the nonverbal and paraverbal aspects of communication, we can get an idea of the dynamics going on in the brain and in the decisions and actions we take.

Once a viral leader has found the right motivation equation for team members and has sprung them into action, the next most valuable thing the viral leader can do is nurture the momentum. Constant communication that takes into consideration the three-signal model will be the critical component to success in this area.

HOW CONFLICT HAPPENS: WHEN VIRALITY GOES WRONG

Let's stop for a moment to consider something that can bring momentum to a halt: conflict. Surveys show that managers can spend 10 to 26 percent of their time dealing with conflict. This, of course, is costly, particularly if the parties involved are not trained to reduce and prevent conflict. We have found that conflict is often an indication of communication problems at the organization. When communication is not clear and when messages are left to different interpretations without considering things like personality type, communication styles, and culture, conflict arises. A focus on building strong communication skills helps us prevent conflict and reduce the cost of dealing with it.

Many of our interactions with others have a neutral function. By this, we mean that at these times, people don't have a hidden intent or agenda behind what they do or say. We are all simply trying to get by and complete our tasks for the day.

For example, we may be walking behind someone on the street who starts to slow down. We say, "Excuse me," and keep on walking past the person. There is no intent to flee from the person; neither is there a desire to get to know them. We are each simply trying to get to our destinations. These simple interactions with neutral functions take up most of our day.

The rest of the time, utilizing a much smaller portion of our day, we work on two other functions. The relational signal helps us build bridges and reach out to others. This side of ours works to bring us together. The relational signal has primarily a uniting function and tries to connect us with those around us to build communities. That is how we build circles of relationships with family, friends, and colleagues.

For example, you may approach prospects with a smile and introduce yourself and then ask them to share something about themselves. Here, you are leveraging biological and relational signals to develop trust and rapport with prospects. The function of the signals is unifying, as you are trying to form bonds with potential customers.

But sometimes, these bonds fail. When this happens, we have conflict—which can sometimes escalate to full-blown confrontation. Why do our bonding efforts fail? There are many reasons, but for now, let's start by taking a closer look at what happens with our biological signal.

As you now know, our biological signal's priority is survival, and a crucial part of survival is avoiding dangers. Our biological side is also often the first filter for what we sense. When we hear, feel, smell, touch, or taste something, the first priority our brains have is to determine if it is safe or dangerous.

When we feel threatened, our biological signal takes over to protect us. Since survival is our top priority, we don't have to think too hard about it.

Instead, our biological responses are often instinctual, automatic, and primal. If something is dangerous, our biological signal distances us from it right away. That's why loud sounds and screams can sometimes make us anxious or even scared. The anxiety we feel is part of our natural reaction, preparing us to protect ourselves in case danger arises. Increased heart rate and faster breathing prepare us to fight our way out of danger or flee from it.

Think about situations that could activate your biological signal: a meeting room that is far too cold or too hot, the sound of two vehicles crashing, a loud alarm, or perhaps the sound of an angry voice. Think of the impact a stressful conversation has on you and your body. Does your heart rate change? How about your breathing?

In cases when we feel threatened, instead of building bridges, the biological signal often prioritizes separating us from the perceived dangers. When a threat is detected, the biological side's primary function is divisive, and building relationship bridges is no longer a priority.

For example, you walk down the street and see a customer who tried to get you in trouble with your manager last week. Your relational signals are strong and you want to mend the situation, but in the customer's mind, the biological signal is strongest, and the individual is determined to fight you and get rid of you by getting you fired. At this point, the client's biological signal's function becomes divisive without the balancing effects of the relational and logical signals.

It is important to note that the biological signal doesn't always carry a dividing function, just as the relational signal doesn't always work in a uniting way. The perception of our circumstances is what determines which direction our actions will take.

Let's review the functions our three signals perform.

FUNCTIONS

→ **Uniting** ←   ♦ **Neutral** ♦   ← **Dividing** →

MONITORING OUR SIGNALS FOR BETTER RESULTS

Now that we understand how we think and make choices, let's see how we can improve our own decisions and influence the decisions of others to achieve better results.

The first questions you should ask yourself here are about how you are reacting to the circumstances around you, using your three signals.

- What messages is your *biological signal* sending? Are you breathing faster than normal, or are you calm? Do you feel safe and assertive or uncomfortable?
- What about your *relational signals*? Is your mind focused on building rapport, or is it focused on you?
- Next, what is your *logical signal* saying to you? Is your logic making your interaction with others cold or routine?

Finally, what is the outcome? Is what you are doing leading to a unifying, a neutral, or a dividing result?

You may have heard old sayings such as "timing is everything" or "location, location, location" that point out factors for success. We submit to you that for viral leaders, the single most important factor for success is *perspective*.

You see, what the world around us is really like matters very little to us. What matters to us is how we *perceive* reality and how it is filtered and decoded by our three signals. **The secret of great leadership and management is mastering the ability to see the world from the perspectives of others**—in other words, to be able to look at the world the way another person does and make sense of it from his or her point of view. Put differently, we need to master our ability to predict and interpret how the three signals influence the other person.

Amazing things can happen when you change your perspective. But when you do, be wise. Don't change perspective for the sake of change alone. Be purposeful and seek the perspectives of leaders. In other words, if you are going to try to look at the world through the eyes of another, put yourself in the shoes of someone you admire. Then, help those around you do the same. That is the essence of viral leadership.

TAKING CONTROL

The next question to ask yourself is, "Can I change my perception of the current situation to generate positive viral leadership?"

You may wonder how we can control the messages that the three signals send our brains and how we can feed the right signal. We often work in projects where success may depend on people we do not directly supervise or where people like customers may cause additional stress. How can we gain control of the signals under those circumstances?

In these situations, we may benefit from making a list of what is and what isn't in our control. For example, we may learn that answering customer calls can cause delays in shipments at the end of the day. While we might not be able to keep customers from calling, we may be able to control calling hours. By opening the phones later or closing calling hours earlier, we could allow ourselves some extra time to work on shipping.

We have full control of what we ask people to do—in other words, the goals we set for the members of our teams. To maximize the successful completion of the goals you set for others, these goals need to meet certain criteria:

CLARITY

A message can be clear to two people in different ways. For example, let's say you are traveling and using your phone for business. During your trip, a client asks you to send your final decision on the title for a book your firm has been editing. You send a text message from your phone to two of your assistants to inform them that your phone's space bar is not working—all the words run together. One of the assistants needs to forward the name of the book to the client. The assistants are not familiar with the account, but they know how to get ahold of the client. You need them to text you back the book title with the correct spaces between words so you can copy and paste it into your response to this very important client as soon as possible.

You send them the title:

hewasoncereal

Where would you place the spaces? Let's see what the assistants did.

Assistant A sends back: "He Was On Cereal," which matches your client's book topic on healthy eating.

Assistant B sends back: "He Was Once Real," which sounds like a play on words for the book (and might also work).

Your instructions were clear. Your message was clear—right? But how each assistant interpreted the message was very different. The lesson here is that a clear goal is one where those implementing it need to interpret it in the same way you intended it. The goal is not clear if it is clear only to you.

How many times have you given instructions (or received them) on your way to the elevator with little time to spare and in a rush? How much time was dedicated to clarity? And how big was the margin for error? If we want to be effective, viral leaders, we need to focus on ensuring that our messages are interpreted as we intend.

Visit the book's companion site viralleaders.com and share with us if you have received instructions that you interpreted in a different way than your supervisor.

VIRAL LEADERSHIP AND HIGH PERFORMANCE

Communicating well with our teams is an effective strategy for getting to know them better and understanding their motivations. It is important to note that when you ask people, "What motivates you?" the automatic answer might be, "A bonus, of course." But now, we know better: we are all biased to think that way—both managers and those we manage. We know that money is rarely the real motivator even though we all assume it is, and that is why we need to make the effort to get to know the people in our teams.

We can be agents for change and initiate motivation even if we are not managers. We do not need to be managers to use our viral leadership skills, and motivating others is a key skill we can continue to develop throughout our careers. We need to think of our work as a lifelong learning experience. What motivates you today may change in a few years. The same happens with your employees and peers as their lives change—as they get married, buy homes, have children, and so forth. All these life changes affect us and our motivations at work.

Our motivations are also influenced greatly by culture. Many of us work with global teams or with individuals from different cultural backgrounds, so we need to monitor our own biases about the motivations of individuals from cultures other than our own.

Let's bring these observations into the workplace. When an individual or a team sets a realistic performance goal, there is a high possibility that the individual or team can achieve more than what is expected. We see this often when teams set stretch goals, which might happen when the team is not yet ready to meet current expectations. The implication is that the team still needs to grow and develop in some way so that it can achieve the goal.

To achieve goals, we need to ensure that we have the right people doing the right jobs. This implies that those involved in the implementation have the knowledge and skill to carry out the plan according to their roles.

Next, everyone needs appropriate levels of access to the necessary tools, resources, and materials to carry out the plan.

Finally, the plan is only viable if enough time is provided to complete it. If too much time passes without action, success may be compromised too.

In the second part of this book, you'll find the SMART goals tool. We recommend that you use it next time you give someone a task. It helps ensure that everyone is clear on the expectations for success and how to achieve success in the most efficient way possible.

BECOMING A CHANGE AGENT

Starting a leadership role with a new company or becoming a first-time leader can be as exciting as it can be challenging.

Many new managers enter situations where the old ways linger and where there is little or no motivation to change. However, as new managers, we may be asked to increase performance or productivity. What can we do when we are responsible for improved results, but the culture of the company isn't ready for change?

We must minimize the impact of divisive messages from our three signals. When teams go through change, they need to adjust. Just as we adjust to becoming new leaders, the team needs to adjust to your new role. Understanding this fear and responding to alleviate it appropriately can help foster a culture conducive to change.

Team members' uncertainty about the future keeps them from feeling vested in change. If they don't know what the future will bring, they fear it. Let's face it. It feels safer and more comfortable to keep things the same. Most people seem to feel better about resisting change than venturing into the unknown.

Our first step toward facilitating change is to build engagement. As you know, motivating teams is hard enough. To motivate them to change is even harder. You'll need to start by removing obstacles such as fear of the unknown. Develop a communication strategy that helps your team understand what to expect during the change period. Clarify what is expected of them (be sure to get feedback about how clear they are on it) and what they are accountable for. These steps will build engagement.

You'll be wise to include your team in the development process where appropriate, so its members understand that their needs are being heard and their opinions have been taken into consideration. Once you build a system of communication and fair accountability, build checkpoints to evaluate progress and monitor staff engagement. Taking these steps to alleviate the team's fears will create an environment that can foster growth and positive change.

CHAPTER 7

STAFF TRAINING: PART OF THE STRATEGIC PLAN

I once tried thinking for an entire day, but I found
it less valuable than one moment of study.
—Xun Zi

Survival in a tough economy is not a matter of chance but rather a matter of careful strategic planning and thorough reassessment of current practices. Competitive strategies need to be developed, and they need to go far beyond having the firm just stay afloat. A critical part of the process includes a long, hard look at how we deal with staff training each year, a rare opportunity to review and revamp staff development and education. Given the circumstances, organizations are remiss not to take advantage of this opportunity.

One fact about an economic crisis (or any other crisis) is that organizations cannot completely stop training staff, just as we cannot just stop marketing or stop spending altogether. We just need to get the most value from how we do these things and be diligent in implementing our revised plans.

Carelessly cutting training budgets without carefully considering mid- and long-term impact on productivity and profitability is just as dangerous as wasting money when the times are good. A leaner time is not the right moment to act with an axe but rather with the precision of a scalpel. Instead of giving in to fear and anxiety, leadership teams and managers need to take these three key steps and then realign staff educational goals accordingly:

- Determine business objectives
- Take purpose-driven steps to eliminate waste
- Reinforce, remediate, and retool

Training is far more than just a way to inform staff. It is a critical component of a comprehensive performance-improvement strategy and perhaps the best delivery vehicle to spread viral leadership.

REALIGNING STAFF EDUCATION WITH BUSINESS OBJECTIVES

Take a look at your organization's business goals and check to see if your education programs are aligned to help you meet them. For example, if one of your goals is to improve profits by reducing billing errors by 3 percent each quarter, you should have a supporting educational solution that addresses the most common billing mistakes your team members run into. If you find that your billing staff is only enrolled in courses for learning advanced e-mail software, you may need to realign your training needs and budget accordingly.

You must answer these questions:

- Do our educational programs and offerings directly support any of our business goals?
- Do these educational offerings help us meet or exceed our objectives?
- What learning offerings do we still need to help our staff meet or exceed our objectives?

One item that is easily forgotten at the start of the fiscal year is that certain updates or changes may require just-in-time training interventions. To avoid last-minute crunches, you should allocate a portion of your budget to education programs designed to maintain necessary updates.

TAKE PURPOSE-DRIVEN STEPS TO ELIMINATE WASTE

Next comes dispensing with all unnecessary training and seeking more efficient ways to deliver and even develop training. E-learning and other methods of distance and asynchronous learning may be better suited to today's conditions. Furthermore, the development of training may be best left to outsourced resources rather than internal staff and managers who need to focus on other aspects of the business.

REINFORCE, REMEDIATE, AND RETOOL

In times of difficulty, stress sets in, and staff members are more likely to be distracted and make mistakes. Your goals and objectives need to be supported by an ongoing, developmental support plan that includes coaching, informal learning, and retraining. There are three reasons for retraining:

- Reinforcing best practices so that the best performers continue to operate at peak performance no matter the circumstances. Reinforcement helps reduce risks associated with performance drift (when people deviate from acceptable work practices).
- Correcting and remediating performance errors and improving low productivity.
- Accounting for lost jobs and employee transitions or departures. Many employees now need to cover open positions while they perform their own regular duties. These staff members need retooling training to support their confidence and to ensure that they are prepared for their new work demands.

WHAT DRIVES AN ORGANIZATION TO IMPROVEMENT THROUGH LEARNING

Recently, we were asked in an online forum about the three most important elements, processes, or systems that drive organizational learning. Though this issue can be analyzed from many angles, the most elemental pieces correspond to the relative strength of an organization.

- In a strong organization, the main focus is often on strategy.
- In a mediocre organization, the main focus is often placed on someone's impetus or impulse.
- In a weak organization, leadership focuses most on reacting to problems or crises.

We find that the best organizations manage their learning initiatives as a very important part of their business strategy and objectives instead of using them to try to put out fires all the time.

To support the organization's strategy, the best organizations put into place these three key elements:

- **The right people.** Put the right learning champion and the right staff together, and let him or her identify the right learners. The right educators are smart enough to identify the right business objectives and then put together the right programs for the right people.
- **The infrastructure.** People need the right tools to do their jobs; otherwise, even the best people are doomed to fail.
- **The support.** From money to time, the learning operation must be supported with real assets. If it isn't, you hire a lot of good people and buy a lot of nice equipment and software but render the team impotent.

PART II

A VIRAL LEADER'S TOOLKIT

If I have seen further than others, it is by
standing upon the shoulders of giants.
—ISAAC NEWTON

One thing we have learned from history is that many great ideas and inventions are nothing more than clever and creative combinations of previous ideas and inventions. Innovation is often the result of combining old knowledge into new formulas.

In our research, we found that several fields of knowledge are aimed at understanding human behavior, and that many experts in these fields are trying to help people achieve better performance. Some of the key fields of study for understanding performance improvement are psychology, education, and business. In fact, these areas of study and research have gained great insight into how to affect behavior and thinking and how to help people achieve more.

Unfortunately, these fields don't always work in collaboration. Sometimes, two of the fields pair their efforts, but we don't usually see all three working together. Why should this matter? Well, just like the blind men who tried to describe what an elephant looked like by describing three different parts of it (the trunk was like a snake, the leg was like a tree, and the tail was like a lizard), without a view that incorporates all three disciplines, we can't see the total picture accurately.

These three fields of study actually intersect at several crucial points—around how people learn, how thinking and behavior can be affected, and improving performance. We want to avoid considering performance improvement from a unilateral point of view. So, in this part of the book, we try to bridge all three fields to gain more clarity. Viral leaders may use this enhanced understanding of performance improvement to maximize their teams' potential.

THE PERFORMANCE-IMPROVEMENT SPECTRUM

When we aim a ray of white light at a prism, it breaks up into a spectrum of colors on the other side. Similarly, let's take what we know about performance improvement and break it into its basic parts. Our spectrum is a set of theories and evidence-based practices developed by experts in business, education, and psychology. Table 1 gives us an idea of how experts approach performance improvement using a combination of sources.

Table 1—Performance-Improvement Spectrum

	Psychology	Education	Business
Business	Marketing, sales, and negotiation experts identify the best ways to influence a buyer's decision. Organizational-development experts seek to improve how organizations function and manage change.	Talent-development specialists focus on how to build employee competencies, how to facilitate transfers of knowledge, and how to improve staff performance.	Business experts focus on how to encourage employee productivity and how to maintain brand loyalty.
Education	Experts in education and psychology research how to improve skill development and lifelong learning.	Adult education focuses on how people learn, retain information, and improve skills and knowledge.	
Psychology	Psychology looks into why and how people think and behave and what influences their thoughts and behavior.		

In each case, the objectives are very similar, and the approaches seem so also. However, each box in the table actually represents a unique point of view. We believe that there are unique characteristics of each combination that may be helpful for the others, but there is no unified model of performance for comparison, analysis, and debate. We believe that a viral leader must create such a unified model. Let's see what it might look like.

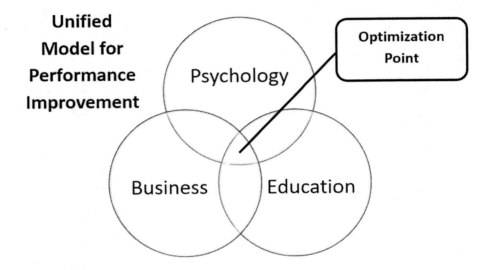

Unified Model for Performance Improvement

Psychology

Optimization Point

Business

Education

If viral leaders combine evidence-based practices from each field of study, he or she can pinpoint sooner what works best to optimize workplace practices. Our goal here is to identify the tools that fall into this optimization point. If you use them effectively, you'll improve your chances of spreading the contagion of viral leadership across your organization.

In the last few decades, organizations have learned much about continuous performance improvement and how to achieve better results consistently. We'll apply some of the principles we have learned from those strategies for helping staff improve its own performance. The three primary tools are ADDIE, SMART, and SWOT. Though you may have encountered them before, here we specifically consider them through the viral leader's perspective.

ACCESS THE VIRAL LEADERSHIP COMPANION TOOLKIT

We offer a companion toolkit with downloadable templates that you can adapt to your own needs at http://viralleaders.com/book-companion-toolkit/

ACHIEVING CLARITY: TRAINING AND ORGANIZATION

In the first part of the book, we stated the importance of achieving clarity to avoid conflict and waste. We also discussed how people who understand their roles and responsibilities are more engaged. To achieve clarity, team members need from their leaders:

- effective training so they understand their jobs and how to do them
- clear plans when engaging in a project

We'll equip you, the viral leader, with the tools to achieve the level of clarity that leads to optimal performance.

THE ADDIE MODEL—A MULTIUSE APPROACH

*You were born to win, but to be a winner, you must
plan to win, prepare to win, and expect to win.*
—ZIG ZIGLAR

The first tool we'll share with you is the ADDIE model. ADDIE stands for

- Analysis
- Design
- Development
- Implementation
- Evaluation

ADDIE does two things: it shows you how to create effective training for your staff, and it helps you plan and manage projects more effectively. The ADDIE model was created originally as an instructional design tool to develop training content. You *can* use this model to plan your next presentation or to create staff training, but it can do much more, including acting as a blueprint for project management. First, we'll look at ADDIE as a tool to develop training, but always keep in mind your goal: to infect your teams with the bug of viral leadership.

Note that ADDIE is an approach and not an exact science. The ADDIE approach is flexible and allows the user, whether a trainer or project manager, to apply different techniques and tools at each step.

Let's look at each of the five ADDIE components in turn.

THE ANALYSIS STAGE

The first part of ADDIE is Analysis. In this stage, you investigate your current circumstances and what you or your team may need to achieve performance improvement. It's like consulting an architect to plan your dream house according to your needs. There are different kinds of analyses that you can do with ADDIE.

GAP ANALYSIS

A gap analysis uncovers the difference between desired and current performance levels. The leadership team should have a clear vision that guides the development of performance goals, and your task is to identify the objectives needed to help staff meet them. Vision, goals, and objectives (VGOs) should give you a clear picture of what the optimal outcome is.

Please note that this step requires careful research to get an accurate measure of the performance gap. You must also have a *way* to measure performance. Not all companies have reliable ways to do this and don't know their performance baselines. You may need to establish some working baselines with available data. Be sure to keep the focus on *measurable* performance, whether learning intervention is meant to cause behavioral or cognitive changes.

RESOURCE ANALYSIS

A resource analysis considers available tools—in this case, those for instructional design and delivery. For example, you may identify the kinds of technology available to you for these tasks. In some companies, all they have is a pad of paper and a marker. Others have complete learning-management-system suites and labs with all the necessary hardware.

You may also want to determine logistical resources, such as training venues, budgets, and so forth. Time is a valuable commodity, and yet we tend to take it for granted. Find out how much time you have available for your targeted audience—and how much time it has for you.

CONTENT ANALYSIS

Content analysis identifies what content is needed, discovering whether content relevant to the need exists, and if you have access to it. If no content exists, then you need to assess if similar content can be adapted or if new content needs to be created. When researching content, ask yourself if there are any limitations, such as copyrights or costs that limit access.

Also assess whether the content fits your overall needs. For example, if you plan to deliver e-learning content via a learning-management system (LMS), ask the following:

- Is all of the content suited for an e-learning format, or should you consider classroom training and practice as well?
- If you're obtaining courses from a vendor, can you customize it to meet your needs?

PEOPLE ANALYSIS

Next, you must consider your people—everyone involved in the development process. Determine who your audience is and what its needs are. Are there obstacles to learning? Are there issues of diversity, accessibility, or any other factors affecting your audience's ability to learn?

Determine which managers will champion the learning initiatives. Make sure to have their support every step of the way and that the team is aware that these champions are behind you and the effort, expecting results.

Finally, ask yourself if there are any other stakeholders you need to contact. If you need the help of subject matter experts (SMEs), make sure to gain their support early in the process.

THE DESIGN STAGE

In the Design stage, you take what you learned from the Analysis stage to build a plan. It's like the stage in designing a home when the architect makes a sketch of the house—it is not yet a blueprint. Things can still change quickly, and we may discover that not everything we had on our wish list is possible in real life. On the other hand, we may also discover that if we make certain adjustments, we don't need everything we originally thought we did.

The best thing you can do as a viral leader at this stage is to remain very flexible. The purpose of this stage is to make your plans as clear as possible. You'll have a clear blueprint, budget, and so on by the end of the design process.

When creating effective training, here are four key components to consider.

STRUCTURE

You can use tools like lesson plans, storyboards, and wireframes to give structure to your content. You should also consider the use of style guides and standardized user interfaces to maintain continuity of design during the development phase.

Another area where structure is helpful is in creating timetables for development and delivery. Here, you look at the project from the perspective of a project manager, ensuring that the right resources and people are available at the right times and allocating responsibilities to the project participants.

VISION

Focus on the VGOs discovered during the analysis phase as you develop a content design and development plan.

Always ask yourself if the section, question, or example you are working on is aligned with its respective objective. Try to get rid of distractions and obstacles that could lead learners away from the key content.

CONTENT

Now that you have identified your content gaps and determined what content is available (or not), it is time to start putting the plan together.

First, align your potential content (or content sources) with your VGOs, leaving out any irrelevant content. Start with already developed content to save time in the development phase later. Then set a development plan for the creation of any outstanding content.

METRICS

The design phase is key to the development of measurable outcomes. As you develop content, you must always think in terms of how you intend to measure it in relationship to its corresponding objective.

Ask yourself how your design will help measure improved performance. Try to build opportunities throughout the learning experience where the learner can receive feedback regarding learning and (when possible) feedback for performance improvement.

THE DEVELOPMENT STAGE

The Development stage is like the one in which an architect and construction crew use blueprints and budgets to build a home. In the creation of training, here is where you write and produce the course content, handbooks, slides, and so on. Generally speaking, Development includes any steps necessary between Design and Implementation. In managing a project, Design and Development are sometimes merged into one step.

Let's explore some key components in the development of effective training.

STRUCTURE

During the design phase, you developed such aspects as content outlines and templates for user interfaces, lesson plans, storyboards, and wireframes. In this phase, you use these tools to structure your learning experience.

You will create other structural elements as well. For example, you may have developed a list of test questions during the design phase; in this phase you determine the order in which they'll appear on the exam. Another task might be to decide on the placements of quizzes or review exercises—after each key content unit, or after a group of them? You will use your intuition as well as experience to make a number of decisions in this stage.

SYNTHESIS

In the analysis stage, you dissected the problem of designing a training program, considering all the interrelated parts. Now, in the development phase, you'll bring them back together. By systematically organizing the learning content to align with your VGOs, you help learners stay focused on the desired performance outcome.

CONTENT

The Development phase is the creative stage. Develop the necessary learning content using the outline created in the design phase. One option is to use Staged Rapid Instructional Development[SM] (SRID). At Learning4Managers.com, we describe this method of developing sections or units of content and then running them through an expedited review and quality assurance process as each unit is complete. Once feedback is received, content is quickly updated and then published. More information in the SRD is available for free and located in the Book Companion Kit Online at http://viralleaders.com/book-companion-toolkit/

ARTISTRY

Artistry is also important in the Development phase. The trick is to find the balance between the art and the science of learning. While the use of visual aids is often encouraged in adult learning, too many graphics can become confusing. Graphics need to be relevant to the content and to augment it, not interfere with it. The same applies to sound effects and music. You must also consider how content is conveyed. For example, metaphors can often help in the learning process, but those that are too obscure may interfere with learning. Always take your audience into consideration. Your gap analysis should help determine any special needs and cultural diversity issues that may be affected by your content.

IMPLEMENTATION

Implementation is when you take your plans into action. In the home-building scenario, this is when you move into your new home. In training, it is the actual delivery of the content to the participants.

Here are four important components in implementing effective training.

TRANSFERENCE

The Implementation phase is the first time the learner is introduced to the output of the Development phase. Implementation is the catalytic step that starts the reaction required for the learning process.

The purpose of the Development phase was to create deliverables to help with the transfer of knowledge and skills to an audience or the refreshment of knowledge and skills. Transference is all about enabling the audience to bring performance up to par with the team's VGOs.

DELIVERY

Delivery of what was created in the Development phase is a means, not an end. People often believe that the instructional designer's job is simply to create learning content and see it through to the point of implementation. They then expect learners to simply take the content in and become proficient, competent, and more productive.

The delivery is only a way for learners to access information and interact with it. The actual act of learning depends strongly on the learner, the learner's circumstances, and the learner's experience with the learning content.

DATA

The Implementation stage is the first introduction of the developed content to the learners and is their first opportunity to retain it. Learners must be encouraged to retain the information, and they should also have the ability to do so. This means allocating sufficient time for review, practice, and acquisition of new knowledge as necessary. This may mean the occasional use of individualized delivery systems for some learners.

OPERATIONS

A variety of factors can affect the effectiveness of implementation. Some may be outside our control, such as availability of extra supplies, on-time shipment, or learning materials that are in faraway locations; power outages; and so forth. An instructional designer should do everything possible to mitigate the possible effects of operational factors, and, when possible, designers should have backup plans for the Implementation phase.

You should also carefully consider the medium in which implementation takes place. For example, if the output is mobile learning via smartphones, do all the learners have access to them, and is the software compatible with all smartphones in use by the learners? Do they have good connectivity? The last thing you want is for learners to feel frustrated with the implementation because of poor connectivity or any other issue not directly related to the learning content itself.

THE EVALUATION STAGE

Finally, we reach the last stage of the ADDIE model. Here is where we assess the outcomes of the implementation. Metaphorically, this would be like realizing, after moving into a new house, that you could have used a spare bedroom, a larger closet, or a smaller stove. The Evaluation stage allows you to determine if your plan worked as you expected and if additional improvements are needed.

Let's take a look at four aspects of evaluation that can help viral leaders ensure that their plans are effective and know where they may need improvement.

EVALUATION OF THE GAP

The gap analysis uncovered the difference between initial and desired performance levels. In the Evaluation phase, we reexamine the gap to see if we have been able to bring optimal and postlearning performance closer together. If the gap in performance persists, then you may need to initiate a new analysis cycle to uncover the nature of the gap's persistence.

Remember that sometimes, certain levels of performance take time to master. Be aware that over time, people can also forget information, leading to deterioration in performance. This latency effect may be countered with ongoing reviews and practice.

VISION

In the Evaluation phase, we can get feedback from the learners after the learning event. Evaluations and performance assessments can help us determine if learners were able to meet the learning objectives and goals. Once again, we go back to VGOs to verify success.

DATA

Data collection and analysis are critical in the Evaluation phase. Make sure that you have clean data and that you evaluate it as objectively as you can. If an individual or a group does not show signs of growth, it does not always mean that you or the learners failed. There may be hidden or even new factors that were not accounted for in the analysis phase of the project.

METRICS

For an evaluation to be of value, you must be measuring the right thing—and apply the right kinds of measurements. Always check your evaluation tools against the analysis and assess whether any changes might have happened between Analysis and Evaluation that could have affected the metrics or the results.

ADDIE AS A PROJECT-MANAGEMENT TOOL—A DYNAMIC MODEL

From Analysis to Evaluation, each step feeds from the last. If done correctly, the entire model loops back, providing feedback for ongoing improvement. As you can see, ADDIE is a powerful approach to instructional design, but it can also aid the planning and design of almost any project. It offers structure and order for the design process and helps ensure systematic development and continuous improvement.

CYCLE OF CONTINUOUS IMPROVEMENT

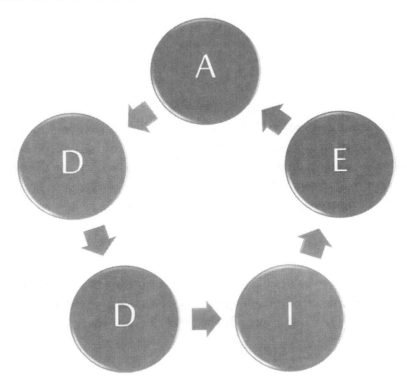

ADDIE AND PROJECT MANAGEMENT

Up to now, we have focused on using ADDIE as a tool to create effective training. But as we mentioned earlier, ADDIE can also help viral leaders build clear plans for their teams. Let's explore how we can use ADDIE to help us with project management.

The first and perhaps most important step at the start of any project is a needs analysis (or needs assessment). Imagine you have a meeting with a client across town and have determined the location and the time. Now, you have a gap to address. How will you reach your destination from your current location on time? To make it to the meeting on time, you plan ahead and figure out the route that best suits your needs and choose a departure time. And, if you are diligent enough, you consider possible delays, detours, and other obstacles you may encounter along the way. This process is analogous to the analysis portion of ADDIE. The needs-analysis process allows us to identify a goal, the gap for reaching it, and a way to address that gap. All your planning for a simple trip across town starts with one key piece of information: your goal, which was to reach a certain place at a specific time. As viral leaders plan for performance improvement and how to maximize their teams' chances of achieving goals, the leaders and their teams need to start by deciding and clarifying what the destination is.

We begin by asking ourselves what the outcome should look like. You may want your salespeople to sell more, or you may want your frontline staff to be more productive. Although those sound like good goals, they are not specific enough. Going back to our trip analogy, imagine your clients telling you that they want to meet you downtown at a restaurant but never deciding on a specific one.

To help you clarify your outcomes, you can use the well-known SMART system for setting goals. SMART stands for *specific, measurable, attainable, realistic,* and *timely.* Goals must be as specific as possible and also measurable, as we noticed in the scenario of planning the directions to a meeting. In this example, you can measure success by arriving on time—or degrees of failure, by how many minutes you are late (or not showing up at all).

Increasing sales is a good goal, but it is more powerful when you specify the types of sales you want to increase, the time frame in which you expect to see the increase, and the percentage of the increase. Setting these parameters will help your staff better understand the effort required to improve their performance. We discuss SMART goals in more detail in the next section.

After you have determined the gap between current and desired performance, you can use the ADDIE design and development templates to guide you through how you and your team will address the need. Brainstorming sessions with your team will help them feel they are part of the creative process and become more engaged in the later stages. Your top priority during this phase is to craft the message you will deliver to your team members in the Implementation phase and to ensure that message is as clear as possible.

When you reach the Implementation phase, the single most important factor for success will be how clearly you communicate the tasks to the team. Finally, once the solution has been implemented, you're in the Evaluation stage. Evaluate your results and adapt your approach accordingly.

SMART GOALS

Productivity is never an accident. It is always the result of a commitment to excellence, intelligent planning, and focused effort.
—Paul J. Meyer

We have mentioned how one of the secrets to the success of viral leaders is their ability to provide clear goals and instructions. They have a clear understanding of their own goals and what they want to achieve. Do you have personal and professional goals? Are you on track to meet them? How do you know?

Ask the average person if he or she has set personal goals. Many people will say they have. But when you ask them to describe their goals in detail, most either hesitate or describe a hope or a dream they have for the future instead of an actual goal. Because people are unclear about what a goal is or how to use goals to help them achieve, we spend a significant amount of time training viral leaders about goal setting.

First, let's be clear about what a goal is. It is a planned achievement that is *specific, measurable, attainable, realistic,* and *timely.* Let's look at an example. Nora is a busy professional who wants to optimize her day. However, her goal is stated as a wish: "I'd like to have more time." Because this wish does not meet the SMART criteria, Nora isn't likely to achieve it.

Let's take that wish and turn it into a SMART goal: "I will free up one extra hour a day next week by creating a time log to track my activities at my desk and at meetings in order to identify which time wasters I can eliminate each day."

Here's a challenge for you: set a SMART goal today! Prepare a personal and a professional goal for yourself by the end of the day.

We use the SMART goal-setting model to help us identify effective goals. It is said that if you can't measure something, you can't control it. SMART goals must be measurable and result oriented. Let's explore the elements of the SMART goal model, of which there have been many versions over the years. We'll explore some of the most common ones.

SPECIFIC: USING A FOCUSED APPROACH

Imagine a group of people learning to shoot a rifle at a faraway target. If the users' scopes are out of focus, they aren't likely to hit the target. An old Latin proverb says, *Si nihil temptes, raro cades.* It is often translated as "If you aim at nothing, you'll seldom miss." A focused goal allows you to pinpoint where and how to spend your efforts.

To help focus your goal, formulate questions that help you define it. For example:

Who are the stakeholders?
What is to be accomplished?
Where are the relevant locations, if any?
When is the project due?
Why do we need to accomplish the goal (what are the benefits)?
How will we approach the problem at hand?

Let's say that Daniel is part of a sales team at a retail store, and he wants to increase sales. He sets a goal that lacks specifics: "I want to increase sales as much as possible." This is too general and lacks focus.

You can be more specific. Let's see what happens with the goal when we answer what, where, how, and why.

- **What:** Increase sales of extended warranties on electronic equipment
- **Where:** At the checkout point
- **How:** By having cashiers promote the extended warranty plans to customers
- **Why:** To engage customers whom the electronics-department staff could not reach or approach to discuss the advantages of the protection plans

MEASURABLE: Keeping Track of Success

To know if he has been successful, Daniel must have some measure of progress. He asks these questions to refine his goal:

- **How much?** By 10 percent
- **How many?**
- **How long?** Over the next twelve months

ATTAINABLE: Engage Motivation

In the first part of the book, we described how the expectation of success motivates people. A successful goal should have an intrinsic call to engage people to act. The right goal also keeps us from pushing so hard that people consider it unachievable. To help us find the right balance, we encourage the use of the final tool in our toolkit: the SWOT analysis, which we'll describe in more detail later.

Our friend, Daniel, could use SWOT analysis to help him see the viability of a goal. Depending on his strengths and the opportunities available at the time, if he tries to increase sales volume by 10 percent over a year, his goal may be doable. However, a 100 percent increase in a day may not be attainable, nor would it feel fair to him or his team.

You may find it interesting to know that George T. Doran is credited with having published one of the earliest versions of the SMART model. In his version, he used "assignable" instead of "attainable": he sees a need to confer ownership of the goal and make the doer accountable for its completion. Other versions of the model use "action oriented" here to emphasize the need to direct people to take action.

REALISTIC: SUCCESS POTENTIAL WITHIN CONTEXT

By now, Daniel knows that he can achieve his goal based on his own skills and abilities, but now he tests the goal by putting it in context. Looking at the desired goal and how it will play out in Daniel's current circumstances helps determine if there are factors conspiring to his failure. Identifying them early can help Daniel avoid or prevent them.

Daniel's goal is to increase sales of extended warranties on electronic equipment, but the checkout team members do not receive formal training on how to sell and promote the benefits of the plans. He realizes that he might not see the best results unless he addresses the issue of training. It is unrealistic to ask people to perform a job well without adequate training and knowledge of the task they are asked to do. The SWOT analysis on weaknesses and threats, which we'll look at soon, will help Daniel identify whether his goals are realistic within his current context or not.

Other versions of the SMART model use the word "relevant" instead of "realistic." In those versions, the focus is on making sure that there is value in the goal for those responsible for accomplishing it. This concept takes us back the motivation equation, where we learned that people are more engaged and motivated when they perceive value in what they do.

TIMELY

This step helps clarify the timeframe for the goal. Daniel could ask questions such as the following:

- What are the start and end dates (if applicable) for the goal?
- How long will this goal last?
- Is the goal's time frame the right one under the current circumstances?

Committing to a start date and monitoring progress toward a goal helps create momentum and nurtures the sustainability of viral leadership efforts.

Other versions of SMART use the word "time-bound" to describe setting a deadline for the goal. Other versions of the model use the word "tangible," meaning that it needs to be something we can experience and measure using our senses of smell, touch, sight, taste, or hearing.

How Viral Leaders use SMART in Coaching

Viral leaders take the time to coach their teams on how to integrate SMART goals into their daily routines. Let's revisit Nora's scenario. She is a new customer-service center supervisor trying to juggle multiple priorities. She feels she doesn't have enough time to do everything, so she has decided that she needs to manage her time better. Linda, Nora's manager, provides Nora with coaching on the use of SMART goals to help her with her time-management issues. Nora walks away with a plan and is ready to develop her first SMART goal. Here is an outline of her approach:

- Write initial goal.
- Check against SMART.
- Rewrite or refine goal.
- Build accountability measures.

Write the Goal

Nora's initial goal looks like this:

I want to manage my time better.

Check against SMART

Nora realizes that her goal does not meet the SMART model criteria and asks Linda for advice. Here is Linda's analysis:

S: Nora's goal lacks *specific* steps.

M: Nora's goal also lacks a description of what she will *measure*.

A: Nora can't determine if she can *achieve* it since she can't measure it.

R: Nora's goal isn't *realistic* if it isn't specific.

T: Nora didn't set any *time* frames to meet the goal.

Let's take a look now at Nora's goal as she refines it, one step at a time, with Linda's help.

REFINEMENT: SPECIFIC

[**What**] I will manage time better [**How**] by creating a time log [**Where**] to track my activities at my desk and at meetings [**Why**] in order to identify patterns and time wasters.

REFINEMENT: MEASURABLE

I will manage time better [**How much**] by finding how to free one extra hour a day by creating a time log [**How long**] for a week to track my activities at my desk and at meetings in order to identify [**How many**] at least three ineffective behavioral patterns and five weekly activities that waste my time.

REFINEMENT: ATTAINABLE

Nora reviews her refined goal to confirm that she feels she can accomplish it. Her strengths in analyzing and identifying patterns can help her accomplish the revised goal, and she feels confident that she can find areas for improvement in her daily routine.

REFINEMENT: REALISTIC

Nora feels confident that her goal is something she can accomplish. She realizes that if she can find patterns in her day, she can combine similar activities and set priorities. She can also identify time wasters she can get rid of and tasks she can delegate. All of these actions can result in time savings, leading to finding that extra free hour a day she needs.

REFINEMENT: TIMELY

Nora can start her time log right away and track every day for a week, and she will catalog patterns by the end of the week. The results are relevant to her ability to achieve the goal.

A FINAL REFINEMENT: ACCOUNTABILITY

Now that she has a SMART goal with targets and deadlines to meet, Nora adds one last layer of security to ensure her success. She asks a mentor at work to keep her accountable and to give her support by checking up on her every day. To keep her motivated, her mentor will offer support and remind Nora of her goal. As a result, Nora is now becoming infected with viral leadership skills and is on her way to becoming a viral leader herself.

SWOT ANALYSIS

All men can see these tactics whereby I conquer, but what none
can see is the strategy out of which victory is evolved.
—Sun Tzu

Developed by Albert S. Humphrey in the 1960s, SWOT analysis is a strategic planning method and the first step in formulating a plan. SWOT is how viral leaders create winning strategies and stay away from efforts that drain them and their teams of time and energy.

SWOT analysis is a great tool to help viral leaders and their teams assess the value of an initiative or a goal. SWOT can help viral leaders identify the low-hanging fruit. It can also help identify where we should not waste our time and effort. When setting SMART goals, SWOT can assist viral leaders determine how viable a goal is and what to avoid to prevent failure.

SWOT stands for the following:

- Strengths
- Weaknesses
- Opportunities
- Threats

Let's take a closer look at each of the SWOT components.

STRENGTHS

You want to identify the internal strengths or advantages that may help you achieve your objective. "Internal" means that they are within your control or the control of your organization. You might find strengths in unexpected places. For example, a small company may appear weak when compared to a large company. However, a small company's strength may be its ability to change direction quickly, whereas a large company is less flexible. Sometimes what appears to be a weakness can be turned into a strength.

WEAKNESSES

Identify the internal weaknesses or disadvantages that may prevent you from achieving your objective. Be fair but honest about weaknesses. This is not the time to pretend that you or your organization are more than what you are.

OPPORTUNITIES

Examine the external advantages or conditions that may help you achieve your objective. "External" means that they exist in the environment you work in and may not be within your control or the control of the organization. Take into consideration social, economic, political, religious, or philosophical factors, among others. An example could be a change in power at your competitor's company or problems with a competitor's supplier.

THREATS

List any external forces or conditions that may prevent you from achieving your objective. Threats to consider could be environmental, social, political, economic, religious, or philosophical, or they could relate to some other condition outside of your control. An example could be a change in sales taxes or the rising cost of fuel for transportation.

SWOT EXPLAINED

WHEN TO USE SWOT

Now that you understand the different elements of SWOT, let's explore the tool even further.

SWOT is used for strategic planning to help viral leaders reach the best possible decisions. As such, it can be used for many purposes. Here are a few examples:

- A local photographer is trying to decide whether or not to use social media to promote her business.
- A company manager tries to decide whether he needs to create a new position or split the work among current employees after closing a new contract.
- An executive of an expanding business explores whether opening an office overseas is the best approach for her company to enter the international arena.

In all these cases, SWOT can help a viral leader determine whether there are forces that push overwhelmingly in one direction or another. The tool also helps viral leaders determine whether these forces can be managed or changed and what approaches can be used to influence these forces.

USING SWOT

Let's put SWOT into practice. Identify a strategy or goal you'd like to assess. Then explore each aspect of SWOT as it relates to the strategy or goal. (The book's companion toolkit gives you a SWOT analysis template that you can adapt to your own needs.)

The first step is to brainstorm ideas about each SWOT component. Start with strengths and then move on to each component in turn. Try to find at least three items in each component so that you end up with a minimum of three strengths, three weaknesses, three opportunities, and three threats. Once you are done brainstorming, narrow your four lists down to a maximum of five top items per list.

As you prepare your analysis, read the tips we provide in this section to help you discover the most relevant SWOT aspects.

STRENGTHS

It is a good idea to brainstorm and identify as many of your strengths as you can. However, once you have a list of your strengths in front of you, try to select the top five that are most relevant to the topic at hand.

Some people find it easier to find weaknesses than strengths. If you find it difficult to identify strengths, try to see where you could turn weakness into strengths. For example, your company may not have a large budget, but you may be able to provide a better response rate than a competitor. Focus on value: the things that matter to you and your customers.

WEAKNESSES

Be honest and don't try to cover up or ignore your weak areas. The last thing you want is to get blindsided by choosing to ignore areas where you were not ready to perform a task. Identifying weaknesses gives you the opportunity to shore up those areas if appropriate. Weaknesses also help us determine whether we should avoid going in certain directions. This is particularly true if a strong weakness is well paired with a strong threat.

For example, imagine an investor planning to invest in a company that produces print products. The investor's biggest weakness is his lack of knowledge of the print industry and of the product's market. Furthermore, the web is a direct threat to the product, and the company has no strategy to migrate to the web. These may be strong signs that it is best to walk away.

OPPORTUNITIES

To identify your best opportunities, consider factors of influence such as your competitors, industry trends, technological advances, legal and regulatory changes, and so forth. If you find it hard to identify opportunities, take a closer look at the external threats. See if you can leverage what appears to be a threat today into an opportunity.

For example, a newsletter company used to printing newsletters might find it difficult to compete with the web. However, if the newsletter has the ability to acquire a smaller online publisher, it could use its unique and copyrighted content and migrate its print content to an online format. The strategy could help the company continue to be profitable.

THREATS

Do not underestimate potential threats. You must also take into consideration future threats. Keep in mind that the threat that may affect you indirectly. For example, the rising cost of fuel affects the cost of transportation, which in turn affects the cost of products. It may be a good idea to enlist the help of consultants or focus groups outside of your company to help you identify threats that might not be obvious to you.

SWOT EXAMPLE

In this example, we'll explore SWOT as it applies to a personal goal. We'll use the template provided in the book companion toolkit.

Mike is planning to purchase a car and would like to assess whether buying a hybrid is a viable option and uses SWOT to help him in his decision process. Let's explore the SWOT assessment along with him.

1. STRENGTHS

When we look for strengths, we look internally. We look for factors that are within our reach or control.

Here is what Mike finds:

- S1. He cares strongly about the environment.
- S2. He has researched the different types of hybrid options on the market.
- S3. His good credit should make it easy to get financing from many sources.
- S4. He has researched the cost of both new and used hybrid cars.
- S5. He works in sales and knows how to negotiate.

2. WEAKNESSES

When we look for weaknesses, we look internally. We look for factors that are within our reach or control.

Here is what Mike finds:

- W1. He knows little about engines and automotive mechanics.
- W2. This is his first experience buying a car on his own.
- W3. He isn't sure he has sufficient funds available for a down payment.
- W4. His current vehicle is in good shape, and he really doesn't need a new car.
- W5. Although he cares about the environment, he cares about his fiancée more. She wants a sport-utility vehicle (SUV).

3. OPPORTUNITIES

When looking for opportunities, look externally. Determine factors in the environment that may be outside your reach or control.

Here is what Mike finds:

- O1. There are many more hybrid choices now than in years past (including SUVs).
- O2. More competition means better prices.

- O3. New technologies make hybrid cars safer, more efficient, and more reliable than before.
- O4. Improved production means less wait time to get a hybrid vehicle.
- O5. There are a few government and dealer incentives available to help finance hybrid vehicles.

4. THREATS

When looking for threats, look externally. Identify environmental factors outside your reach or control.

Here is what Mike finds:

- T1. Some research suggests that hybrid fuel-cost savings may not make up for initial investment.
- T2. Some banks won't finance hybrid vehicles.
- T3. Mike lives far from the closest dealership that sells and services hybrids.
- T4. Incentives to buy hybrids may not be available if the economy worsens.
- T5. New fuel-efficient vehicles are priced competitively, keeping hybrids expensive in comparison.

SWOT AND MIN-MAX

As a last step, you'll explore the relationship between the different findings from your SWOT analysis with a min-max review, enhancing the value of your analysis.

Your objective is to minimize failure and maximize success (min-max) by identifying:

- Strengths and opportunities that support one another;
- Opportunities that may reduce the effect of weaknesses;
- Strengths that may reduce the effect of threats; and
- Internal weaknesses that may be supported by external threats.

THE MIN-MAX ADVANTAGE

The relationship between the different SWOT components allows us to find where our competitive advantages are.

- Strength and Opportunity (SO) findings show us our best success potential.
- Strength and Threat (ST) observations show us our best growth opportunities.
- Weaknesses and Opportunity (WO) are a sign of potential distractions.
- Weaknesses and Threats (WT) is our danger zone. We should avoid this area at all costs.

Use your findings to help you take maximum advantage of your strengths and opportunities. Use what you have learned to make necessary adjustments to counter any weaknesses and threats. Keep in mind that leverage may be achieved with minor adjustments. For example, assume response time has been identified as a threat. You would want your sales staff to be able to access data for potential customers faster and while on the road. Today, you provide basic phones and a basic phone plan for your traveling sales force; however, upgrading your employees' mobile devices and services may help them gain access to the data they need in a timelier manner.

SWOT AND MIN-MAX EXAMPLE

Rachel is a new manager who has been tasked with improving the company's website performance. Customers have complained that the site is too slow and takes a long time to load page content and images. Rachel decides to use SWOT to determine what strategy she needs to adopt.

After brainstorming, Rachel identifies the following:

1. **Strengths**
   - S1. The website is becoming more popular, and more people are coming to it every day.

- S2. Using an external website-host vendor keeps site-maintenance costs low.
- S3. Online orders continue to rise every month.
- S4. The website-hosting contract is scalable and allows Rachel to buy more bandwidth and space.
- S5. Recent upgrades to the site (like adding video demos) have drawn more people to it.

2. **Weaknesses**
   - W1. There are no website experts in house.
   - W2. Customer reviews reveal that the site is slow.
   - W3. The website-host vendor claims it cannot replicate the problems that customers see.
   - W4. Continuing website-traffic growth contributes to the site's slower performance.
   - W5. Recently added videos to the site contribute to slowing down the site's performance.

3. **Opportunities**
   - O1. Adding videos to the site has potential to help the site take advantage of viral marketing.
   - O2. Current industry forecast predicts 25 percent traffic growth to the website in twelve months.
   - O3. Website-hosting services costs have declined in the last year.
   - O4. Research indicates that customers with a positive online experience tend to return.
   - O5. Research indicates that customers with a positive online experience tend to send referrals.

4. **Threats**
   - T1. Competitor sites are starting to mirror the features of Rachel's site.
   - T2. Continued growth will eventually slow the site to a halt unless it is upgraded.

- T3. Growing complaints can lead to losing potential customers more rapidly.
- T4. While traffic growth to the site is expected, it cannot be predicted with 100 percent certainty.
- T5. Additional website-hosting costs may cut into profits.

Min-Max

In the min-max review, we consult the combined areas of inquiry as described above. For this example, we have paired particular items (e.g., Strength S5 with Opportunity O1) to show how they add together.

SO: Areas to Pursue

S5O1: The new videos on the site have helped increase traffic by going viral. Rachel can consult with host vendors to see whether there is a way to host the videos on a different site to spread the load and to keep the main site from slowing down or if there is a way to optimize the current site to stream videos.

S4O3: Decreasing hosting costs and the availability of scalable services may indicate that it is time to renegotiate their web-hosting contract. Rachel may ask if there is a way to manage the site to dynamically update bandwidth to manage higher loads when there is higher demand and use of the site.

ST: Observations for Growth

S1T3: Increasing numbers of new customers on the site make it imperative to create a positive customer experience. This alone should justify increased spending in faster hosting services.

S3T5: While upgrading the hosting services may cost more, calculations indicate that sales revenue far surpasses these costs and offsets any investment in upgrades.

WO: Distractions to Prevent

W1O2: Constant increases in web traffic may necessitate a better in-house knowledge of how to attract new customers while maintaining sustainable services. Before the SWOT analysis, Rachel was only looking at technological upgrades. Now, she is considering bringing some additional expertise in house.

WT: Aspects to Avoid

W4T2: Rachel does not want the site to be a victim of its own success. The more traffic the company's website gets, the quicker the site could fail. Future solutions need to be dynamic and need to be able to account for traffic fluctuations.

THE TOOLKIT IN ACTION

In order to carry a positive action we must develop here a positive vision.
—DALAI LAMA

Our intent at the start of the book was to help new and experienced managers become viral leaders with positive traits and skills they can quickly transmit to the team members such leaders work with.

The tools we provided you in this kit, ADDIE, SMART, and SWOT, are a starting point for you to become the viral leader you want to be. Using these tools can help you create a culture of viral leadership in your organization, where you can start an epidemic of leadership and performance improvement. Now it is up to you to start putting the tools to work.

Earlier, we discussed how viral leaders are able to maximize effectiveness by giving their teams clear messages and expectations. To be able to give clear expectations, viral leaders must first be clear about what they expect from their teams. Clear communication removes the fear and confusion that creates inaction. Clarity also helps prevent conflict and increases productivity.

Use the tools in this toolkit to create the level of clarity for yourself and your teams that leads to action. As a result, you'll find your resolve strengthened and your teams more engaged than ever before.

Get Started

- Select a project you are currently working on or one you want to begin.
- Use the ADDIE templates to organize all the information about the project. The templates will help you organize your thinking and to create a clear picture for you and your team of what is expected.
- Use the SMART goal templates to create a set of goals designed for success.
- Use the SWOT analysis template throughout your strategy-development process to help maximize your potential for success.

Tips

- Remember to watch for motivation suppressors in yourself and in others.
- Make sure to address people's needs by balancing the biological, relational, and logical signals.
- Check regularly whether your message is creating unity or being divisive.

CONCLUSION

Thou hast seen nothing yet.
—Miguel de Cervantes Saavedra, *Don Quixote*

At the start of our journey, we talked about Eric and Laura and their struggles while transitioning into management and leadership roles. They are not alone. Many professionals and entrepreneurs across the world struggle in the same way, trying to make sense of their roles.

Leading a team is a great responsibility, and guiding a team to optimal performance can sometimes appear like an unsurmountable challenge. Many people give up and leave management and leadership roles feeling defeated and wondering why they did not just stay where they were prior to their last promotion.

This tragedy can be averted, and people like Eric, Laura, and you can indeed become viral leaders. It isn't always easy, but the process is simple. The tools and ideas we have shared here are only the beginning. Success will depend more than anything else on the fortitude of spirit that each person brings with him- or herself.

You may not feel strong now. If that's the case, don't despair. Just take one step, then the next, and then one more. As you gain momentum, soon you'll feel something inside you changing. But you have to make the decision to believe in yourself and choose to become the viral leader you want to be.

Throughout the book, we have given you opportunities to assess yourself and your own virality. Now it is time to take action. Are you a viral leader? If not, what steps will you take today to help you become one? We support you, and we want to hear from you. Join us on our website and tell us your success stories.

http://ViralLeaders.com

Follow us on Facebook:
https://www.facebook.com/viralleaders

Our final tip is this: never stop learning, and encourage everyone you meet to continue to grow and develop through training. The more we learn, the greater viral leader we become, and the more infectious we are. Spread the word! Spread positive viral leadership.

We thank you and wish you the best.

ABOUT ACCOLADE INSTITUTE, INC.

Accolade Institute, Inc. was founded on the premise that today's emerging leaders, managers, supervisors, and entrepreneurs are not satisfied with being good enough or average. They want to become great at what they do, and they want to make a difference. They want high-powered teams with high-performing team members. Finally, they also want highly engaged customers.

The founder of the company realized throughout the late 1990s and early 2000s that a great challenge in the training world was the lack of evidence-based information about what works and what doesn't. Organizations struggled with training materials that were dated, didn't encourage engagement, and produced marginal results. Leaders searched constantly for the best tools available, only to find the same old, unimaginative, and uninspired content.

Learning4Managers.com was created as a division of Accolade Institute, Inc. for the sole purpose of offering relevant and engaging training based on current research and evidence-based data. From our early beginnings, we knew that it was time to challenge old training paradigms and time to create a new generation of training and development for today's emerging leaders. Now is the right time for training and development to evolve, and from the start, Accolade Institute, Inc. has decided to take a leading role in the process.

ABOUT THE AUTHOR

Jorge Acuña, MEd, MBA, is passionate about helping emerging and established leaders become great at what they do. For over fifteen years, he has dedicated himself to researching how to optimize human performance and maximize engagement through effective learning practices. A known authority in leadership development, every year he provides customized training and consultation services to thousands of clients around the world, from entrepreneurial businesses to multibillion-dollar global enterprises.

During Mr. Acuña's experiences as a global learning strategist, he has dedicated himself to researching how to optimize human performance and maximize engagement through effective learning.

Mr. Acuña has observed that, given the right tools, guidance, and encouragement, individuals can perform and achieve beyond their own expectations. Mr. Acuña's passion is to pass his knowledge on to others as he practices and models the same principles he has learned. To see his clients increase revenue and pride in what they do as a result of his work is one of his greatest rewards.

Mr. Acuña's philosophy is, "If the people you encounter treat you like gold, then treat them like diamonds!" His desire is to help emerging and established leaders become great at what they do. He is often described as a "welcoming individual" and a "great problem solver." His personalized approach to facilitation is matched by his analytical-thinking ability and his desire to bring the highest possible value to every minute his clients spend with him.

CPSIA information can be obtained at www.ICGtesting.com
Printed in the USA
LVOW10s2248120416

483339LV00011B/141/P